Photo by Eusebio Rojas Guzmán

OCTAVIO PAZ

Homage to the Poet

Edited and with an Introduction by Kosrof Chantikian

KOSMOS
San Francisco
1980

"Nocturno de San Ildefonso"/"Nocturne of San Ildefonso" as translated by José L. Varela-Ibarra is published by permission of New Directions, Publishers of Octavio Paz, *A Draft of Shadows and other Poems*, © 1979 by Octavio Paz and Eliot Weinberger.

"Rappaccini's Daughter" as translated by Harry Haskell is published by permission of Octavio Paz, copyright © 1956, 1980 by Octavio Paz.

"Himachal Pradesh (2)" and "Custodia" (from *Ladera este*) and "Movimiento"/"Movement" (from *Salamandra*) as translated by Robert Lima are published by permission of New Directions, copyright © 1969, 1972 by Octavio Paz.

The excerpts from *Viento entero* by Octavio Paz are reprinted by permission of New Directions, copyright © 1971 by New Directions Publishing Corporation.

Library of Congress Catalog Card Number: 80-82167

ISBN: 0-916426-03-3

Published simultaneously as a special double issue of *KOSMOS: A Journal of Poetry*, No. 5–6 / Spring-Summer and Autumn-Winter 1980 / Homage to Octavio Paz.

This project was partially supported by funding from the National Endowment for the Arts.

KOSMOS
2580 Polk Street
San Francisco, CA 94109
USA

CONTENTS

FOREWORD

I am indebted to all those who made the birth of this *homenaje* possible.

Jaime Alazraki's article is a translation of "Para una poética del silencio," from *Cuadernos Hispanoamericanos* (Madrid, Enero-Marzo 1979)—a special triple issue devoted to Paz; Yves Bonnefoy's poem is the title section of *Dans le leurre du seuil* and appears in the U.S. for the first time; Claude Esteban's article is a translation of "De la poésie comme insurrection," from his introduction to *Versant est* (1978)—the French edition of *Ladera este*—and appears in English for the first time; Edwin Honig's conversation with Octavio Paz first appeared in a slightly longer version in *Modern Language Notes* (October, 1976) and was also published in its present form in *New Boston Review* (Spring, 1976); José Miguel Oviedo's discussion of *Pasado en claro* ("Los pasos de la memoria: Lectura de un poema de Octavio Paz") was first published in *Revista de Occidente* (Diciembre, 1976); Anthony Rudolf's interview (which he edited and translated from the French) took place in Cambridge, England in 1971 and was first published in a slightly different form in *Modern Poetry in Translation* (Autumn, 1971); the short bibliography is taken from Hugo Verani's "Hacia la bibliografía de Octavio Paz," which also appeared in the aforementioned issue of *Cuadernos Hispanoamericanos*. With the exception of the "Nocturne of San Ildefonso" translated by José L. Varela-Ibarra and "Himachal Pradesh (2)," "Custodia" and "Movement" translated by Robert Lima, all translations of Octavio Paz's poetry are my own.

I am very grateful to Katharine Hermann who, during the seventeen months it took to invent this book, gave me her invaluable help and encouragement and energy throughout the manuscript's preparation.

Finally, my thanks to Octavio Paz for his generosity, his humor, his poetry: A Poet whose Work perpetually reinvents himself, language and ourselves every day. A Poet who in his adolescence heard the voice of the Devil and immediately intuited the truth that "Energy is Eternal Delight"; and that in the process of inventing the poem, the poem simultaneously invents, transmutes and metamorphosizes the Poet into one who comprehends, above all else, the essential significance of ourselves as beings whose deepest foundation is Love.

—*KC, San Francisco, June 1980*

1

Kosrof Chantikian

THE POETRY AND THOUGHT OF OCTAVIO PAZ
AN INTRODUCTION

I The Poet

In his foreword to the first edition of *El arco y la lira*[1]
(The Bow and the Lyre), Octavio Paz puts a question to us
and to himself: "From the time when I began to write poems,
I wondered whether it was worth while to do so: would it not
be better to transform life into poetry than to make poetry from
life?" Like all authentic questions, this is really an invitation
for us to enter into a living dialogue with the Poet. And like
all true questions, the shadow of an answer is already implicit
within it. Let us ask then what Paz's question means for us.

In an essay delivered in 1942, "Poesía de soledad y
poesía de comunión" ("Poetry of Solitude and Poetry of
Communion"), Paz declared that "poetry is neither moral
nor immoral, just nor unjust, false nor true, beautiful nor
ugly. It is, simply, poetry of solitude or of communion"
(PO, 99–100). This is an astonishing statement for Paz to
have made before an audience gathered in Mexico City to
celebrate the fourth centenary of the birth of San Juan de la
Cruz. And perhaps Paz felt a little strange saying this because
several pages on in the essay, he plainly contradicts himself:
Poetry, he says, is nevertheless a great force which reveals to
us our hidden longings and dreams and allows us to actualize
them. The Poet, by teaching us what our dreams are (and in
fact demonstrating that *we have dreams*), shows us at the
same time that we are not simply machines created for the
purpose of following commands or spilling blood "to enrich
the powerful or to maintain injustice in power" and that we
are more than mere statistics or pieces of goods that can be
inventoried. And poetry in directly manifesting these dreams
"invites us to rebellion, to live our dreams awake: to be no

---

[1] *El arco y la lira* (Mexico, 3rd ed. 1972), p. 7. Paz's works are abbreviated as follows: *AL: El arco y la lira; PO: Las peras del olmo* (Barcelona, 2nd ed. 1974); *CD: Conjunciones y disyunciones* (Mexico, 1969); *CA: Corriente alterna* (Mexico, 1967); *LPB: Libertad bajo palabra* (Mexico, 2nd ed. 1968).

3

longer the dreamers, but the dream itself" (*PO*, 105).

Can such a *force*, an invention of the soul of such magnitude that it teaches us to invent ourselves and even if necessary to rebel, can such a poetry be called "neither moral nor immoral, just nor unjust, false nor true, beautiful nor ugly"? Can a poetry which declares *dream what you might be,* can such a poetry be not committed to a higher vision of our potential? And can a poetry which reveals to us our hidden depths, which teaches us about ourselves, and which therefore embraces and advances a consciousness of superior authenticity, can such a poetry be *other than* moral and just? Can we not therefore legitimately call such a poetry true and beautiful? Paz himself acknowledges that *El arco y la lira* is the maturing and correction of his "distant" essay, but we are warned that his question ("Would it not be better to transform life into poetry than to make poetry from life?") is not to be taken as a proposal to make life more beautiful. Guillermo Sucre, for example, paraphrasing Paz, declares "Life is neither beautiful nor ugly, noble nor ignoble."[2] Sucre adds that Paz is proposing instead to have everyone base their lives on the principle of poetry—where contraries are fused into a unity, where contradictions become resolved, where fragmentation is healed and where dichotomy is finally negated.

Let us note first here that "life" is what we invent for ourselves out of ourselves. This inventing of life is an act, it has the force of intentionality, a consciousness behind it. It is therefore a *value*: One chooses to live in *this way* rather than in another way, to be this type of person rather than that type. This entails a commitment whose freedom is the foundation of the act. To make the claim as Sucre does, that life is neither beautiful nor ugly is already to have committed himself to a particular value. A pretending not to take a stand, not to make a decision, is already to have acted. Neutrality, like the denial of freedom, is an illusion, a self-deception, a lie. It is therefore clear that we have a right to judge whether certain acts undertaken in our inventing ourselves and one another may be called "good" or "bad,"

---

[2] "Octavio Paz: Poetics of Vivacity," in *The Perpetual Present: The Poetry and Prose of Octavio Paz*, ed. by Ivar Ivask (Norman, Okla., 1973), p. 8.

"reasonable" or "fanatical," "beautiful" or "ugly."

To say that life is neither this nor that is a verbal confusion. "Life" refers to human beings who create, invent, discover themselves in this world, who act and interact, who speak and are spoken to, who listen and are listened to, who touch and are touched, who commune and participate with others, who are transfigured by the world and who in turn transfigure it. "Life" is time in the historical continuum out of which all of us arise; the sum total of our acts from our birth, our first movements as conscious beings, to our last, to our death. Thus the structure of action which posits itself through an intentionality, a freedom, a consciousness, can never possess a neutrality. Furthermore, what could it possibly mean to say that Poetry (whose fundamental foundations are the Imagination, Possibility, Eroticism and Love) governs our experience except that utopia has been found? Being a construction of the Imagination and Will, the act of founding this utopia *is a value.* What shall we name this value? Beautiful! Sucre is thus mistaken when he claims that Paz's question has nothing to do with "life": with its beauty or ugliness, its sublimity or wretchedness.

Paz himself understands this very well when he points out that all great poets at one time or another have believed in a revolutionary, libertarian society which would at last resolve the contradictory tensions between the simultaneous affirmation and negation of history perpetually residing in the center of the Poem's Being (*AL,* 254). In this revolutionary society poetry would finally become, as Lautréamont predicted in his *Poésies,* practical and for *everyone!* Since the reformation and critique of language must be the basis of the reconstruction of philosophy and thought, the very *least* that would occur in such a community is the creation of a pure Language! Would such a new Language, the speaking of it purely, transform our lives, make it that is, "more beautiful"? Of course it would! Thinking's foundation *is* Language. A pure Language would be unrestrained, liberating, free of bureaucratic jargon, and unmanipulative as Orwell prophesied. In such a sustaining environment thinking and intuition would more closely approach their potentiality to re-create ourselves through a genuine self-consciousness, a consciousness, that is, no longer chained, muzzled and entombed. This gain in a pure

Language (or at least the *movement toward it*) then would obviously be the beginnings of the creation of utopia.

In such a society consciousness would undergo a metamorphosis, a transfiguration: the transcending of linear time and the overthrow of a history of mutilation into a new time, a *present,* where love is neither a solitary instance nor an accident nor a stroke of luck, but an awaking to the Poetic Instant, the present, here, today. This present, as Paz says, is what poets and artists continually seek even though they are not always aware of it (*CD,* 142). And how will we know this present, this new time? "Perhaps," Paz says, "the alliance of poetry and rebellion will give us a vision of it" (*CD,* 142–43). This merging of poetry and rebellion must be possible only because there exists an affinity between the two. What is this affinity, this analogy, between poetry and rebellion? First, authentic poetry (as all true art) reveals to us the *hidden:* poetry places our consciousness above the usual noise of chatter, it reveals the *other* to us; in so doing, poetry rips off the mask that hides the world by re-creation of the world as a *presence.* Rebellion also reveals the world to us because its function is to demystify society.[3] Both poetry and rebellion destroy deception; both are subversive to the established norms; both transform the given reality; both are a criticism of society: of its myth of progress, of linear time, of language.

Against Sartre who claims that literature is an illusion, that we never live as well as we might dream or write about living, Paz observes we have no choice: we are human because of language: "Living implies speaking and without speech humankind cannot have a full life. Poetry, which is the perfection of speech—language speaking to itself—is an invitation to enjoy the whole of life" (*CA,* 189–90). What then is the basis of this invitation from poetry? From where does it arise? Let me repeat: to enjoy the fullness of life must mean to live in such a way that not only am I happy—but you, the *other,* the shadow of myself, are also happy. A world without poetry is logically possible, but morally, aesthetically, a contradiction. Who would want to live in that hell? Isn't this

---

[3] Herbert Marcuse, *The Aesthetic Dimension: Toward a Critique of Marxist Aesthetics,* trans. by Herbert Marcuse and Erica Sherover (Boston, 1978), pp. 7, 56.

proof that poetry is an essential ingredient of our soul? Moreover, doesn't the very concept of "living a full life," a life
based on authenticity, entail "truth" and "beauty"? Poetry
sustains and nourishes the Imagination; it raises consciousness, as Rimbaud would have said, to a higher power; and because of its living energy and erotic tension, poetry reminds
us of *life*, of a superior way to be, of the power of love, of
who we are and who we may become.

   C. M. Bowra has pointed out in his preface to Paz's
Anthology of Mexican Poetry that a nation's character may
be deduced from its poetry, what it has sought to preserve as
a true reflection of its spirit. Thus, poetry, or rather the poem
which is a *work*, contains within itself a universe of experience: of a "poplar of water" or of gas ovens, of a reminder
that love will never die or of torture. "To love is to struggle,"
says the Poet, "and if two people kiss / the world is transformed." Poetry and the experience found in the poem, a
work, is always more than the artist intended: the poem, any
work of art, is a living being, always independent of its creator. We can see this in any of Paz's great works, in *Piedra de
sol*, for example:

> amar es combatir, si dos se besan
> el mundo cambia . . .
>   . . .
> amar es combatir, es abrir puertas,
> dejar de ser fantasma con un número
> a perpetua cadena condenado
> por un amo sin rostro;
>   el mundo cambia
> si dos se miran y se reconocen,
> amar es desnudarse de los nombres
>   . . .
> . . . mejor ser lapidado
> en las plazas que dar vuelta a la noria
> que exprime la sustancia de la vida,
> cambia la eternidad en horas huecas,
> los minutos en cárceles, el tiempo
> en monedas de cobre y mierda abstracta
>   (*LPB*, 248–49)

(to love is to struggle, and if two people kiss
the world is transformed . . .

. . .

to love is to struggle, to open the doors
to stop being a ghost to a number
condemned to life imprisonment
by a faceless master;

                                   the world is transformed
if two people look at and recognize each other,
to love is to rid ourselves of names

. . .

better to be stoned to death
in the town square than tread the mill
that squeezes life's substance dry,
turns eternity into empty hours,
minutes into prisons, and time
into copper pennies and abstract shit).

The meaning of this fragment from *Piedra de sol* (as in any
work of art) is the *image* and only the image (*AL,* 109–10).
And though it is futile to try to "explain" a poem, it is also
true that the poet and artist believe their "images tell us something about the world and about ourselves and that this something . . . really reveals to us who we are" (*AL,* 107–8). This
is precisely the aesthetic power of a great art and within it lies
a *force* capable of disclosing to us the lost secret of a time in
which humankind had not yet severed itself from being at one
with the universe: *wisdom.* The poem is thus a negation, a
criticism, of the world's reification and an attempt to represent the actual goal of rebellion (and revolution): liberation
and happiness of the individual.[4] The subversive nature of
the poem is not based merely on the knowledge of things, of
the world, which it puts before us in its re-creation of reality,
though that is certainly true; it is rather, something much
more. The poem is subversive because its foundation, medi-
ated by experience, is a "higher knowing": *wisdom.* This
wisdom from which the true poem is born is the reason it is
able, through the image, to tell us about the world and reveal

---

[4] *Ibid.,* p. 69

to us ourselves: the elemental power of the poem, in this sense, is of the same undiminished magnitude as Socrates' moral dictum: *Know Thyself.*

Our question which all artists conscious of their work and of the historical continuum in which we all live, create and transform the world (and are in turn transformed by) must eventually face, is answered as soon as it is posed. We'll see that rather than being antagonistic and irreconcilable, the two elements of our question (transforming life into poetry—making poetry from life), because of their dialectical nature, are inseparably intertwined and converge upon one another relentlessly, having the same tendencies, characteristics and functions: to change, transmute, reshape, metamorphosize and revolutionize the given.

Though it is true to say that we choose ourselves, we decide who we are and who we will become, it is equally true that this freedom-of-Being has a certain intrinsic, inescapable relation with necessity, with the world: the unavoidability of a Poet being a Poet. One chooses to be a Poet, it is true; but the Poet who chooses must choose. How could it be otherwise? This contradiction worries philosophers and they sometimes have nightmares over it. For it is they who have chosen to regard analytical reason rather than the Imagination as the sole unifying principle of the world. They forget, these professors, that after class they will return to their homes, converse with a friend, exchange thoughts, intuit feelings, make love, touch the night, dream. These events and their participation in them: are they capable of being reduced to a deductive logic, a mathematical identity, an *a priori* truth?

The contradiction of choosing to be and simultaneously having to be a Poet can be put in a more general way: Finding ourselves surrounded *by* and *as history* and therefore being formed by it, how much is it possible to poetically create ourselves and thus to invent History? Dreams of transforming life into poetry vs. making poetry out of life: are not these ultimately the same processes? Is not the first dream simply the other side of the second?

What is it to say we will transform life into poetry but another way of speaking of change, metamorphosis, transmutation and revolution? And the Poem: what is its function except to return us to the origin of time (our childhood), the beginning of beginnings (our birth), the starting point of our Being (consciousness of our authentic experience), all of which take place at once, now, here, this instant?

Poetry does this by negation, alchemy, magic, desire, eroticism, by daring language to sing, and by singing—existing. In other words, by destroying history in order to find, that is, to compose, to invent History. Unlike the existing situation today where history (worship of a technology and "progress" that sputters forth its specter of ideological tentacles and bureaucratic control) daily conditions a petrified conscious-ness into its grave, this new History will be one born, nour-ished, comprehended and so actually invented and shaped by a Consciousness immediately and spontaneously aware of its intentionality.

This Consciousness is another way of speaking of the new Person who will be born in History; who will appear by a negation and destruction of the presently dominant form of (a masochistic-sadistic) consciousness. Consciousness will now create History instead of history overpowering, enslav-ing, terrorizing consciousness. But this is precisely the goal of revolutionary Marxism: to dismantle the existing super-structure of society, to destroy a "false consciousness" and to transform history into History, into universal socialism; to make, in other words, the new Person.

The revolutionary Being of Poetry is its ability through its own directive to authentically ground our Being-in-the-world, to throw ourselves out-of-our-selves so we may be able to fundamentally comprehend our existence, so that we may essentially and supremely recognize ourselves as be-ings whose deepest recesses and foundation is Love. The task of humanity is to restore to itself, to recapture, above all to remember its original Being—now lost, buried, forgotten in its frenzied "pursuit of happiness," in its insatiable hunger for more technology, for "progress," in its lust to conquer nature. Until that time when our original Being (which is the Being-of-Love) is restored to us, it is only Poetry which will allow us to comprehend in a truly fundamental way the Being toward which we must become (*AL*, 37).

Paz's thoughts parallel Heidegger's,[5] whose own dialogues with Hölderlin and Rilke emphasize that the being of existence

10

is the being of song. In his third *Sonnets to Orpheus,* Rilke says: *Gesang ist Dasein*—Song is Existence (Part I). Rilke's Imagination which has equated authentic song with authentic existence undermines the established norms of society. "Song is Existence" is a revolutionary declaration. It renounces technology which cannot commune either with nature or ourselves; it laughs at the religion of ideology (politics); it is the disinfectant for the abscess of bureaucracy. Thus Poetry which is grounded and arises from Language-Thought-History, from the Imagination, is revolutionary.

Poets and other artists who understand this revolutionary, transmuting, erotic, subversive (and necessary) element of art cannot disown their work without destroying themselves. And it is Paz himself who reminds us that the Poet and the Poem are one[6]: how could Baudelaire be Baudelaire apart from his poems? (*CA,* 191). Poets who abandon Poetry abandon themselves. Poets who write "verse" for the state will end up themselves as enforcers of ossified codes, as mere functionaries of a bureaucratic, frozen ideology, as bullies. Memory will not allow us to forget the murders, suicides, tortures and silencing of Poets. Whoever condemns Poetry condemns in the same breath the sky and the air; whoever condemns Poetry also condemns at the same time the possibility of a general revolt against petrification of the human spirit. Poetry and revolt must come to meet, to share one another's presence. Let there be no doubt however, that it is the Poet who prophesies this communion.

Paz's question with which we began: "Would it not be better to transform life into poetry than to make poetry from life?" has haunted him since he began to write. The implication is not solely an aesthetic judgment, but is also a moral one: that it would be "better" to give up creating poems and instead change life, the world, into poetry. But how can we transform the world into poetry? How is it possible to create a universal Poetic Consciousness? The very being of society

---

[5] Martin Heidegger, *Poetry, Language, Thought,* trans. by Albert Hofstadter (New York, 1971).

[6] "Introduction to the History of Mexican Poetry," in *An Anthology of Mexican Poetry,* ed. by Octavio Paz and trans. by Samuel Beckett, with a preface by C. M. Bowra (Bloomington, Ind., 1965), p. 43. *PO,* 32.

is anti-poetic. Poetry has no exchange value in society. It is looked upon as impractical, useless. How then shall we negate existing society and reshape it into a Creative Community of Beings, each of whom is *autonomous,* each of whom is both *law-maker* and *law-obeyer* in this new society? The underlying catalyst can only be either a persistent application of pressure for gradual reform (including rebellion) or a more sudden, catastrophic, upheaval—revolution, since the being-of-society is deeply antagonistic to the Being-of-Poetry. (Paz chooses rebellion over the violent excesses evoked by modern revolutions.)

Furthermore, a Poetic Community which implies an Autonomous Community is irreconcilable with existing history. An Autonomous Poetic Community is the destruction of this history into a History. Implicit in Paz's question is thus a value judgment: transformation of society into a Poetic Community is more important (that is, "better") than a mere creation of poetry from a world which at the present moment is, among other things, filled with brutality, murder, hunger, poverty, disease and ignorance.

Paz's question is a dialectic: each element of which attempts to break away, to flee, to suck up the other, but cannot because each is contained in the other: first, the beginning of the transformation of life into poetry is the invention of a Poetic Consciousness, a return to original time before fragmentation severed the unity of the world's Being, before a dichotomy arose between Freedom and Existence, Reason and Imagination, Love and Eroticism, Culture and Society, Art and Work, Work and Pleasure. . . . And second, the creation of poetry from life is the opening up of Possibility, unleashing the full revolutionary and erotic potential of the Imagination into a metamorphosis: of the given into a Creative Community, of history into a History and of consciousness into a Consciousness which at last directs and is the foundation of History.

We have said that the Poet cannot abandon Poetry without being destroyed. Let us for the sake of argument assume this is now possible. Poets will renounce the inventing of poems and instead, transfer all their energies toward the reconstruction of life into poetry. I ask: with Poetry abandoned how will we *know* Poetry? How will we recognize it? Since life is to be transformed into Poetry, it is obvious we need to remember what Poetry was, how it existed, in order to *know how to make life into it!* How will life know it has become poetic with Poetry under embargo? From the past? But what is the point of returning to the past if we abandon Poetry in *our own time?*

This situation collapses upon itself: in order to create (life as) Poetry, we abandon (the making of) Poetry; in order to make life poetic (which is really to say: in order to make life more *human*—since the history of the world is the history of Language, and so thinking), we turn away from song, from dance, away from existence! How then will poetic life dwell if the Imagination is forsaken?

To pose our question, I said earlier, is already to have answered it because a questioning, a looking, a touching, a writing (of a poem, a book) can never be an empty or neutral event. To pose a question is to hope, to desire contact, to commune with another human being, to commit ourselves to a value, *to act.* Paz returns to his (and our) question near the end of *El arco y la lira* (*AL,* 253–54). His answer is quite a natural outcome of the dialectical being of the question: it is *impossible to choose between* Society and Poetry, between Life and Language, between Existence and Song. Each is the umbilical cord and source of the other. Society without Language would be like a body without a heart, a being in search of a brain. Such a society not only would hardly be worth preserving, it could not exist. No one would speak. And Language without society—how is this even conceivable? Language is what makes society possible. It is, according to Heidegger, the dwelling place of Being, that which gathers everything into itself and then returns every being to its own self.[7]

To transform life, existence, society, from its common, stupid, painful being, into the Creative Being of a Poem; or to create Poetry from the presence from which it must be born: the choice is neither one nor the other. It would not be a choice! As soon as one attempted to isolate, to separate, to mutilate, to take one from the other, both would simultaneously vanish (like a collision between a particle and its anti-

---

[7] Heidegger, pp. 100, 132.

13

particle). Poetry is Language, purely, originally. A society that abolished Poetry would be committing in the same act suicide. To condemn Poetry is to condemn Language and as a consequence, thinking!

Between Doing and Being; between Knowing and Being; between the Evening and Morning Star; between the Imagination and the Body—how do we "choose"?

II The Poetry

Eruption, woman, nakedness, embrace, blood, dust and ashes, death, abandons, world, leaves, pomegranate trees, noon, sun and moon, water, air, fire, earth, stars, flying, bodies, you, we, language, words, dreams, time, history, autumn, night, breast, existence, eyes, silence, solitude, the empty space of writing.

To discover the inventions and language of Paz is to experience a primordial beginning of ourself, a return to the origin of the world, a relearning of our forgotten erotic dances, of the Imagination venturing to the abyss in order to arrive at an open space where it will touch Song and Existence, where Body becomes Imagination.

In *Libertad bajo palabra,* a collection of five volumes of Paz's poetry, we find an inexhaustible energy moving simultaneously through dimensions of thinking and feeling with a magnitude of the spectrum of autumn colors. One of these poems "Hacia el poema" ("Toward the Poem") is from the volume *¿Águila o sol? (Eagle or Sun?):*

I

Damos vueltas y vueltas en el vientre animal, en el vientre mineral, en el vientre temporal. Encontrar la salida: el poema.

. . .

Arrancar las máscaras de la fantasía, clavar una pica en el centro sensible: provocar la erupción.

Cortar el cordón umbilical, matar bien a la Madre: crimen que el poeta moderno cometió por todos, en nombre de todos. Toca al nuevo poeta descubrir a la Mujer.

. . .

14

II

Palabras, frases, sílabas, astros que giran alrededor de un
centro fijo. Dos cuerpos, muchos seres que se encuentran
en una palabra. El papel se cubre de letras indelebles,
que nadie dijo, que nadie dictó, que han caído allí y
arden y queman y se apagan. Así pues, existe la poesía,
el amor existe. Y si yo no existo, existes tú.

. . .

El poema prepara un orden amoroso. Preveo un hombre-
sol y una mujer-luna, el uno libre de su poder, la otra
libre de su esclavitud, y amores implacables rayando el
espacio negro. Todo ha de ceder a esas águilas
incandescentes.

. . .

Todo poema se cumple a expensas del poeta.

. . .

Cuando la Historia duerme, habla en sueños: en la frente
del pueblo dormido el poema es una constelación de
sangre. Cuando la Historia despierta, la imagen se hace
acto, acontece el poema: la poesía entra en acción.

Merece lo que sueñas.

(LBP, 205-7)

I

We turn and turn in the animal belly, in the mineral
belly, in the belly of time. To find the way out: the
poem.

. . .

To tear away the masks of fantasy, to drive a lance into
the nerve center: to incite the eruption.

To cut the umbilical cord, to kill the Mother: crime the
modern poet has committed for all, in the name of all:
It is up to the new poet to discover Woman.

. . .

II

Words, phrases, syllables, stars which turn about a fixed
point. Two bodies, many beings that find each other in
a word. The paper is covered by indelible letters, that

no one said, no one pronounced, that have fallen there
and blaze and burn up and die out. In this way, poetry
exists, love exists. And if I do not exist, you do.

. . .

The poem prepares a loving order. I foresee a man-sun
and a woman-moon, he free of his power, she free of
her slavery, and implacable love streaking through black
space. Everything must give way before these incandescent eagles.

. . .

Every poem is realized at the poet's expense.

. . .

When History sleeps, it speaks in dreams: on the brow
of a sleeping people the poem is a constellation of blood.
When History wakes, the image becomes act, the poem
happens: poetry moves into action.

Deserve what you dream.

This is a poem not so much *of* exploration, every good
poem is certainly that and incalculably more. It is the being-
of-exploration: between the Poet and Time, Time and History,
History and Language, Language and the Poet. As always the
beginning is the belly, the womb, the starting place, the point
of departure. And it is by and through the elemental unit of
the phrase this poem will begin, be upheld and continue. Only
Language which begins our journey can take us to the opening, the threshold, the world, into existence. But if it is necessary to cut the umbilical cord which has given us life and the
strength to begin our journey of becoming, why must the
modern Poet commit murder in the process? How is this
crime committed in the name of us all? And who or what is
the Mother being killed?

The answer is tradition, history, ideology, Christianity.
A severing of eternal time, of paradise, of tradition, is accomplished, a necessary act, so that History may become the beginning of the future—which is now, this moment, the Present.
The new Poet is the first who will rediscover Woman. It is
Woman who has been buried 5,000 years by a patriarchal
consciousness. In discovering Woman, the Prophetic Poet discovers the other side of our world, that lost part of ourselves,

that part killed, made silent, ridiculed, neglected; that element of the world, *yin*, without which its contrary and complement, *yang*, cannot exist: History, Wisdom.

This is the Poet's relation, obsession and yearning for original time, the beginning before the world was tempted by a lust to seize control of Nature, before fear and hatred had become an excuse to acquire power over another; a time before the discovery of inauthenticity, stupidity and inequality. This original time will be once again, now: original time-future time and future time-original time:

> The poem prepares a loving order. I foresee a man-sun and a woman-moon, he free of his power, she free of her slavery, and implacable love streaking through black space. Everything must give way before these incandescent eagles.

It would be a mistake here to think that man is only sun (reason-thinking) and woman only moon (intuition-emotion). Thinking-emotion (reason-intuition) are another of a pair of contraries which cannot exist separately. The unifying tension and force which require Thinking and Emotion, Intuition and Reason, Sun and Moon, Man and Woman, Desire and Knowledge, Freedom and Necessity, Energy and Delight to indissolubly embrace is the same as that which for us invents the universe: the Poetic Possibility of the Human Imagination.

The sublime strength, high tension and erotic quality in the language of this great Poet has still not found its potential audience in the North. Of his poetry, only *Early Poems, Configurations, Eagle or Sun?, Renga: A Chain of Poems* (a collaboration with Jacques Roubaud, Eduardo Sanguineti and Charles Tomlinson), and *A Draft of Shadows* have been translated and published in book form here. In fact, more of Paz's critical writings abound in English than his poetry (see prose works, pages 244–45).

Paz's insatiable mind which extends to philosophy, anthropology, linguistics and literary and art criticism tends to overshadow his poetry. But it is for his poetry that he first attracted attention and it is his poetry which of all his writings is most unique. It is above all, his poetry which for us matters most:

Allá, donde terminan las fronteras, los caminos se borran.
Donde empieza el silencio. Avanzo lentamente y pueblo
la noche de estrellas, de palabras, de la respiración de un
agua remota que me espera donde comienza el alba.

Invento la víspera, la noche . . .
. . .
Allá, donde los caminos se borran, donde acaba el silencio, invento la desesperación, la mente que me concibe,
la mano que me dibuja, el ojo que me descubre. Invento
al amigo que me inventa, mi semejante; y a la mujer, mi
contrario . . .

Contra el silencio y el bullicio invento la Palabra, libertad
que se inventa y me inventa cada día.

(LBP, 9–10)

Over there, where frontiers end, the roads are erased.
Where silence begins. I advance slowly and I people the
night with stars, with words, with the breathing of a remote water that waits for me where the dawn begins.

I invent the evening, the night . . .
. . .
Over there, where roads are erased, where silence ends,
I invent passion, the mind which conceives me, the hand
which designs me, the eye which discovers me. I invent
the friend who invents me, my counterpart; and woman,
my contrary . . .

Against the silence and noise I invent the Word, freedom
which invents itself and invents me every day.

In Octavio Paz we have found what has been forgotten
in our day: the Poem and the Poet are the same. If we are
told it is the Poet who sits down at a desk to create, to fash-
ion phrases into the living being of a Poem, I will add that it
is the Poem which causes the Poet to invent those phrases
which the Poem will become. The freedom of the Poet—the
Poet's Imagination—creates, shapes, invents, transforms, metamorphosizes the Poet in this very act. To our list of contraries
which require themselves to exist only when their complementary elements have a like presence in the world, we must

add Poet-Poem.

Against silence and noise (each a movement and negation into the other) Paz invents the Poem, aware that it is always the Freedom of the Poem which invents himself and us everyday. Language: words, phrases, poems, become the being of thought, passion, song; and in turn, invent Language which discovers itself, and allows us to discover ourselves. Language –Thought–Freedom–Song–Existence–Language. Each is for the other, each discovers and invents the other.

Paz's origin and thus source of strength is Mexico: place of Toltec Pyramids, Aztec gods, land of Spanish subjugation, U.S. domination; a nation looking for its past with its arms flung open to "progress." If it is this Mexico which has partly invented him, as all of us are invented in one way or another by a collective history, a unique time and place, it is also his prophetic vision, his dialectical language, his contradictory tensions and his lyrical eroticism all interwoven at once, here, now into a *Presence,* into a whole tapestry of Being which has made him a universally great Poet–one who easily transcends the stupid boundaries and arbitrary divisions of land masses still archaically called "nations."

III The Poet–The Poetry

It is the Poet who in a time of destitution, a time that is, when the world is so destitute it has little awareness even of its destitution, journeys to the abyss, experiences it, comprehends it and returns with a vision, a warning: either the world must fundamentally turn away from this abyss or annihilate itself. It is the Poet's task to venture to the abyss because only the Poet is venturesome and daring enough to do so. Dante descends into hell while still a mortal in order to comprehend how and where he went astray from the true path, to recapture his original being and to recount his experiences to us so we may know of the dangers of living inauthentically, of fragmenting ourselves from the world.

Society must learn to listen to the prophetic voice of its Poets. Hölderlin, who first poses this question in his poem "Brod und Wein" ("Bread and Wine"): ". . . und wozu Dichter in dürftiger Zeit?" (". . . and what are Poets for in a destitute time?") brings us full circle back again to our question:

19

"Would it not be better to transform life into poetry than to make poetry from life?"

In Nature, in the world's original time, there was no contradiction between Love and Eroticism, Reason and Intuition, Being and Authenticity, Desire and Knowledge, Action and Thought, Community and Creativity. But today the world is split up. Original time has been lost, forgotten, mutilated. Nature has been conquered by tools. Adolescents carry calculators to school but have no knowledge, no comprehension of the foundations of mathematics. Imagination is an orphan, unwanted, called impractical, and treated as a vestigial oddity having no utility. And thought vitiated gives birth to that twin mutation, technology and "progress," a hydra difficult to extirpate. Is it therefore utopian to conceive that society can be transformed into an integrated Poetic Being and that Love will undergo a genuine metamorphosis—rediscovering its authentic Being, its eroticism?

Paz is echoing the revolutionary prophecy of Lautréamont when he said that *poetry should be made a "practical truth" for everyone,* and Rimbaud, when he declared that *Love needed to be reinvented!* Will everyone create poetry? Can Love undergo a fundamental transformation? Each question (and therefore the answer given it) is contained in the other.

Poetry is a revolutionary vocation because its deepest foundation is Love; and Love in its original state is equivalent to the Erotic in our authentic Being in Nature (original time). Thus Love and Eroticism, which are inseparable from each other and commune by virtue of the Imagination are the original subversive elements in the world. Until a time comes (and it will) when society is metamorphosized into one where history's negation has become a *History* being invented and directed by Consciousness, Poetry will remain practically the only avenue open for the world to comprehend itself. I have said and let me repeat—that it is for this reason, if no other, that true Poets can never abandon Poetry without eventually destroying themselves. (The case of Rimbaud, one of our greatest Poets, is no exception. After abandoning poetry at nineteen his life ever after was, as his letters show us, one of constant worry, self-doubt and pity, drifting from one place to the next until his death at thirty-seven.)

Poetry is the Imagination and the Body together, Desire and Knowledge, Pleasure and Work, Love and Eroticism, Intuition and Reason, Sun and Moon, Knowing and Being, Existence and Song, Venture and Daring, Action and Thought, Energy and Delight, Life and Language, Freedom and Necessity.

Our goal is and will always be both Society and Song; and because Song is, as Rilke has said, the same as Being, it is the Poet who teaches us who we are, who we may become, from where we have traveled and even, through the magic and power of prophecy, that Poetry and History will someday embrace. Husserl once remarked that philosophers were the civil servants of Humanity. I will add: Poets are its Soul!

San Francisco
1977–1980

☆ ☆ ☆

Octavio Paz

NOCTURNE OF SAN ILDEFONSO

1

Inside the space of my window, night invents
                                        another night,
another space:
                        trembling celebration
inside a square yard of darkness.
                                        Momentary
alliances of fire,
                        nomadic geometries,
wandering numbers.
                        From yellow to green to red
the spiral uncoils.
                        Window:
magnetized film of messages and responses,
high voltage calligraphy,
falsified heaven/hell of industry
over the changing skin of an instant.

Signs/seeds:
                        the night shooting them off
rising,
        exploding up there,
                                falling
already burnt,
                in a cone of shadows,
                                        they reappear,
rambling lights,
                clusters of syllables,
gyrating fires,
                they disperse,
                                fragments again.
The city invents and nullifies them.

I am at the entrance of a tunnel.
These lines drill holes in time.
Perhaps I am the one waiting at the other end of the tunnel.
I speak with my eyes shut.
                              Someone
has planted in my eyelids
a grove of magnetic needles,
                        someone
guides this line of words.
                        The page
has become an ant's nest.
                        The void
has found itself a place in the pit of my stomach.
                                              I fall
endlessly over this void.
                        I fall without falling.
My hands are cold,
                  my feet cold
—but those alphabets burn, burn.
                              Space
makes and unmakes itself.
                        Night insists,
night touches my face,
                        touches my thoughts.
Wanting what?

                              2

Empty streets, one-eyed lights.
                        On a corner
the specter of a dog
                        searches in the garbage
for the ghost of a bone.

Agitated cockpit:
neighborhood yard and its Aztec dance.
                              Mexico, around 1931.
Street hummingbirds,
                  a flock of children
with unsold newspapers
                        build a nest.
The streetlights invent
                      in the dark loneliness
unreal pools of yellowish light.
                              Ghostly appearances,
time opens:
            a lusty, dismal sound of heels:
under a *sooty sky*
                  the flame of a skirt.
C'est la mort—ou la morte . . .
                              The indifferent wind
tears wounded posters on the walls.

At this hour
            the red walls of San Ildefonso
are black and breathing:
                              sun turned into time
time into stone
              stone into body.
These streets were once canals.
                              Under the sun,
the houses were silver:
                        city of lime and stone,
moon fallen in the lake.
                        The white men raised,
over the drained canal and the buried idol,
another city

    —not white: pink and gold—
idea turned into space, tangible number.
          They placed it
on the intersection of the eight directions,
            its doors
opened to the invisible:
       heaven and hell.

Sleeping neighborhood.
      We walk through galleries of echoes,
among broken images:
       our history.
Silent nation of stones.
        Churches,
vegetation of domes,
       their fronts
petrified gardens of symbols.
        Engorged
in the rancorous proliferation of dwarf homes,
humiliated palaces,
       fountains without water,
dishonored facades.
      Heaps,
white corals without substance:
         piling up
over the seriously-ill massive structures,
        conquered
not by the sadness of the passing years
but by the shame of the present.

Plaza del Zócalo,
vast as the heavens:
                    transparent space
court of echoes.
                    There we invented,
with Aliocha K. and Julián S.
                              meteoric destinies
to face this century and its armies.
                              We are pulled
by the wind of thought
                    the verbal wind
the wind that plays with mirrors
                              lord of reflections
builder of cities of air
                    geometries
suspended by the string of reason.

                              Giant worms:
unlit yellow streetcars.
                    S's and z's:
an insane car, insect of evil eyes.
                              Ideas
fruits within hands reach.
                    Fruits: stars.
                              They burn.
It burns, the powder tree,
                    the adolescent dialogue
suddenly burned out frame.
                    12 times
strikes the bronze fist of the towers.
                              Night
shatters into pieces,
                    later gathers them and herself,

26

unharmed, and becomes one.
                              We part,
not there on the plaza with its worn out trolleycars,
                                                  here,
on this page: petrified letters.

3

The young man who walks through this poem,
between San Ildefonso and the Zócalo,
is the man who writes it:
                              this page
is also an evening walk.
                              Here incarnate
the specter friends,
                    the ideas disappear.

Good, we wanted good:
                         to set the world straight.
We didn't lack strength:
                         we lacked humility.
What we wanted, we didn't want innocently enough.
Precepts and concepts,
                         theologians' pride:
strike with the cross,
                         found with blood,
build the house with bricks of crime,
decree obligatory communion.
                              Some
became secretaries of the secretaries
of the General Secretary of Hell.

                    Anger
became a philosopher,
                    its drool has covered the planet.
Reason came down to earth
and took the shape of a scaffold
                    —and millions adore it.

Circular confusion:
                    we have all been,
in the Great Theatre of the Gutter,
judges, executioners, victims, witnesses,
                                    we all
have borne false testimony
                    against others
and against ourselves.
                    And the worst: we were
the public who applauds or yawns in its seat.
Guilt which does not know itself to be guilt,
                                    innocence,
was the greatest guilt.
                    Each year was a mountain of bones.

Conversions, retractions, excommunications,
reconciliations, apostasies, recantations,
zigzag of devil worshipping and andro-worshipping,
bewitchments and detours:
my history,
            are they the histories of a mistake?
History is the mistake.
                    Truth is that,
beyond dates,
            this side of names,

that which history despises:
                        this day
—anonymous heartbeat of us all,
                        heartbeat
unique to each of us—,
                        the unrepeatable
each day identical to every day.
                        Truth
is the essence of time without history.
                        The weight
of the weightless instant:
                        stones under sun,
seen very long ago and returning today,
stones of time which are also of stone
under this sun of time,
sun born on a day without a date,
                        sun
that lights up these words,
                        sun of words
that darkens when we say them.
                        They burn and go out
suns, words, stones:
                        the instant burns them
without burning itself.
                        Hidden, at rest, untouchable,
the present—not its presences—always is.

Between doing and seeing,
                        action or contemplation,
I chose to act on words:
                        to make them, inhabit them,
give eyes to language.

Poetry is not truth:
it is the resurrection of presences,
                                    history
transformed into the truth of undated time.

Poetry,
        like history, is made;
                            poetry,
        like truth, is seen.
                    Poetry:
                            incarnation
of the sun-over-the-stones in a name,
                                    dissolution
of the name into a reality beyond stones.

Poetry
        hanging bridge between history and truth
is not a road to this or that:
                            it's seeing
the stillness in the movement
                            the movement
in the stillness.
                History is the road:
it leads nowhere,
                    we are all on the road,
truth is to keep on going.
                        We neither go nor come:
we are in the hands of time.
                        Truth:
to know ourselves to be,
                        from the beginning,
                                        suspended.
Fraternity over the void.

30

4

Ideas vanish,
           specters remain:
the truth of what we lived and suffered.
An almost empty taste remains:
                    time
—shared passion—
           time
—shared oblivion—
             at last transformed
into memory and its incarnations.
                    All that remains
is time turned flesh given out: language.

Inside my window,
            war games,
                  turning off and on
the commercial heavens of advertising.
                  Beyond,
barely visible,
           the true constellations.
Between water tanks, antennas, rooftops,
liquid column,
         the moon
              more mental than physical,
cascade of silence,
         appears.
             Neither ghost nor idea:
once a goddess and now wandering light.

My wife sleeps.
          She is also moon,
light that flows
          —not between cloud reefs,
between the rocks and the sorrows of dreams:
she is also soul.
          She flows under her closed eyes,
from her forehead she falls,
                    silent torrent,
to her feet,
          over herself she drops
and from herself she gushes,
                    her heartbeats sculpt her,
she invents herself as she travels over herself
she copies herself as she invents herself
between the islands of her breasts
                    she is an inlet of the sea
her belly is the lake
          where shadow and its vegetations
vanish,
     she flows through her figure,
she rises,
     she falls,
          over herself she spreads,
                    she ties
herself to her flow,
          she disperses herself in her form:
she is also body.
          Truth
is the waves of breathing
and the visions seen by shut eyes:
evident mystery of the person.

Night is about to overflow.

                                 Light breaks.

The horizon has become watery.

                                 To jump

off the height of this hour:

                            to die

will it be to fall or to rise,

                              a sensation or a cessation?

I close my eyes

                     I hear inside my skull

the steps of my blood

                     I hear

time going through my temples.

                              I am still alive.

The room has filled with moondust.

                            Woman:

fountain of the night.

                    I place my trust in your peaceful flow.

from Vuelta
trans. by José L. Varela-Ibarra

RAPPACCINI'S DAUGHTER

PLAYERS
(In Order of Appearance)

THE MESSENGER

ISABEL — *an old servant*

JUAN — *a student from Naples*

RAPPACCINI — *a famous doctor*

BEATRICE — *his daughter*

BAGLIONI — *a doctor at the university*

Prologue

*The garden of Doctor Rappaccini. Seen in the fore-
ground is a section of an old building where we
find Juan's room. The scene will be set up so that
the spectators will see only the interior of the habi-
tation: high and narrow, a large mirror covered with
dust, a desolate atmosphere, a balcony—seen through
a deteriorated curtain—opening up to the garden.
In the center of the garden stands a fantastic tree.
As the curtain rises, the stage remains dark, except
where* THE MESSENGER *is standing, a hermaphroditic character dressed like one of the Tarot figures,
but not resembling any one in particular.*

MESSENGER

My name? It does not matter. Nor my origin. In reality I
don't have a name, nor sex, age nor land. Man or woman;
child or adult; yesterday or tomorrow; north or south; the
two genders, the three times, the four ages and the four cardinal points converge in me and in me dissolve. My soul is transparent, if you look into it you will be submerged in a cold and
dizzy clarity; at the bottom you will find nothing that is mine.

Nothing except the image of your own desire, until now unknown to you. I am the meeting place, in me all roads come to an end. Space, null and void. I am here and there; everything is here, everything is there. I am in any electrical point in space, in any magnetized point in time: yesterday is today; tomorrow, today; everything that was and everything that will be, is taking place at this moment, here in this land or there, in the star. The encounter: two glances that merge until they become an incandescent point, two desires that embrace and form a bond of flames. The encounter, freely accepted, fatally chosen.

Unions and separations: souls that unite and form a constellation that sings for an instant in the center of time, worlds that break apart like the seeds of a pomegranate spread out over the earth.

He takes out a Tarot card.

And here we have the center of the dance, the fixed star: the nocturnal queen, the infernal lady, the woman who governs the growth of the plants, the rhythm of the tides and the movements of the sky; the lunar hunter, the shepherd of the dead in the subterranean valleys; the mother of the harvest and the springs, alternately golden and dark, who sleeps half the year and awakens clothed in bracelets of water; in her right hand the solar wheat of resurrection.

He takes out two cards.

And here we have the enemies: the King of this world, sitting on his throne of manure and money, the book of laws and the code of ethics upon his trembling knees, the whip within the reach of his hand. The King of justice and virtue, who renders unto Caesar what is Caesar's and denies the Spirit what is of the Spirit; in front of him, the Hermit: idolator of the triangle and the sphere, scholar of Chaldean writings and mute in the language of the blood, lost in his labyrinth of syllogisms, prisoner of himself.

He takes out another card.

And here we have the juggler, the adolescent; asleep, his head resting upon his own infancy. He hears the nocturnal song of the lady and awakes. Guided by the song, he walks toward the abyss with his eyes closed in search of his dream; his footsteps are leading toward me, who does not exist; if he weakens he will fall over the precipice. And here we have the last card:

the Lovers. Two figures, one the color of night, the other the
color of day. Two roads. Love is choice: life or death.
   THE MESSENGER *exits.*

Scene I

*The garden remains in shadows. The room is dimly
lit; the curtain of the balcony is closed.*

ISABEL
Entering and showing the room.
At last, young man, we have arrived.
   Reacting to his disturbing silence.
It's many years since someone lived here, that's why there is
sadness in the air. But you will give it life. The walls are
large . . .

JUAN
Perhaps too large. So high and thick . . .

ISABEL
That way the noise won't enter from the street. Nothing better for a student.

JUAN
So gloomy and damp. It won't be easy getting used to this
humidity and silence, though it has been said that solitude
strengthens thought.

ISABEL
I assure you that in no time at all you'll feel right at home.

JUAN
In Naples my room was large and my bed high and spacious
like a ship. Every night, when I closed my eyes, I'd navigate
through seas without names, undiscovered lands, continents
of shadow and foam. At times the thought of never coming
back would terrify me and I would see myself lost forever in
the depths of a black ocean; but quietly, faithfully, my bed
would slip over the edge of night and every morning I would
be deposited on the same happy shore. I slept with the win-

dow open; at dawn the sun and the breezes from the sea would enter my room.

ISABEL

In Padua there's no sea, but we have the most beautiful gardens in all Italy.

JUAN
To himself.
Sea and the sun above the sea. This room is too dark.

ISABEL

Because the curtains are closed. When they're open the light will blind you.
She opens the curtains; the garden appears before the audience, illuminated.

JUAN
Dazzled.
Well, that's better. What golden light.
He crosses to the baclony.
And there's a garden: does it belong to the house?

ISABEL

Years ago it formed part of the palace. Now it belongs to the famous Doctor Rappaccini.

JUAN
Looking over the balcony.
That's not a garden. Not a Neapolitan garden. It's a nightmare.

ISABEL

That's what a lot of people say in Padua, sir. But don't be alarmed; Doctor Rappaccini doesn't cultivate ordinary flowers; what you see are medicinal herbs and plants.

JUAN

Nevertheless, the air is delicious. It's cool and then warm, light, subtle; it's not heavy and there's hardly a trace of perfume. I have to admit that Rappaccini might not know anything about pleasing the eye but he sure knows the secret of perfume. What kind of man is he?

ISABEL

I've already told you. A scholar, a true scholar. They say that there is no other doctor like him. And other things . . .

JUAN

What kind of things?

ISABEL

You will have to judge for yourself. Today or tomorrow you will see him from the balcony; he comes out every day to look after his plants. Sometimes his daughter is with him.

JUAN

I don't like it.
He closes the curtain.
And the daughter, is she like her father?

ISABEL

Beatrice is one of the most beautiful creatures these old eyes have seen. Many have tried to court her, but from a distance, because her father won't let them come close. And she is shy: she flees at the sight of a stranger. Can I offer you anything else, sir? I will be happy to serve you in whatever way I can. You're so young and handsome. And you seem so alone . . .

JUAN

No, thank you, Madam Isabel. Solitude is not dangerous.
ISABEL *exits.*

Scene II

JUAN

I shall try to get used to this cave. Provided that I don't turn into a bat.
He goes over to the mirror and blows away a layer of dust; he makes gestures imitating the flight of a bat; he laughs; becomes serious. At that moment Isabel enters, which startles him.

ISABEL

Excuse the interruption, sir. I felt terrible leaving you all alone so I decided to bring you a bouquet of roses. Maybe they will cheer you up. I cut them myself this morning.

JUAN
Receives the flowers.
Thank you, Madam Isabel.
ISABEL *exits.*

JUAN
What a beautiful gesture. They're lovely, but I have no one to
give them to.
*He hurls them into the air; then smiles, picks them
up, approaches the mirror, looks very pleased with
himself, bows, offers the flowers to an imaginary
girl and pirouettes. Immobile, he hesitates: then
jumps up, opens the curtains and looks over the
balcony. He spots Rappaccini, and bends down so
he can observe without being seen.*

Scene III

RAPPACCINI
Examining the plants. He leans over a flower.
All that I have to do is look at you and you blush like a timid
girl. What sensitivity! And what a flirt! You're blushing but
you're well protected: if someone touches you, he will soon
find his skin covered with a thick vegetation of blue stains.
He jumps up and spots two other plants, entwined.
The loving ones, embracing like an adulterous couple.
He separates them and pulls one out by its roots.
Now you are alone but your violent passion will produce, in
the one that scents you, an endless delirium, like a thirst: delirium of mirrors.
He jumps up and sees another plant.
Are you life or death?
He shrugs his shoulders.
Who knows? And isn't it the same? When we are born, our
bodies begin to die; when we die, we begin to live . . . with a
different life. Who would dare say a cadaver is lifeless? The
worms? They would reply that they have never enjoyed better health. Poison and antidotes: one and the same. Belladonna,

hemlock, agua tofana, henbane, hellebore. What an infinite
variety of forms and effects! Lacteal poison, impudent bala-
nus, the mist, white goosefoot, the hypocritical coral insect,
puffballs and Satan's ticket . . . And by his side, separated by
barely an inch on the scale of the species, the lycopodium and
pneumonia, the oriental musk and the domestic mold, terror
of the cooks. Nevertheless, the principle is the same: a small
change is sufficient, a slight alteration, and the poison is transformed into an elixir of life. Death and life: names, names!
He stands up next to the tree.
Beatrice, my daughter!

BEATRICE
Enters through the door and advances.
Here I am, father.

RAPPACCINI
Look how our tree has grown. Every day higher and more
graceful. And covered with fruit.

BEATRICE
In front of the tree.
How beautiful, how handsome! My, you have grown, my
brother.
She embraces it, placing her cheek against the trunk.
You don't speak, but you respond in your own way; your sap
quickens.
To her father.
I can hear its pulse, as if it were alive.

RAPPACCINI
It is alive.

BEATRICE
I meant to say like you and me. Alive like a boy.
She holds a leaf and inhales it.
Let me breathe in your perfume and steal some of your fire!

RAPPACCINI
I was just thinking: what is life for some is death for others.
We see only half of the sphere. But the sphere is made of life
and death. If I could approach it with the right measures and
proportions, I could instill portions of life in death; then the

40

two halves could unite: we would be like gods. If my experiment . . .

BEATRICE
No, don't talk to me about that! I am content with my fate
and happy in this garden, with these plants: my only family.
But still at times I would like to hold a rose and smell it; put
jasmine in my hair; pick the petals of a daisy, without them
burning my hands.

RAPPACCINI
Roses, daisies, violets, carnations, plants that wilt in the frost,
flowers that lose their petals in a light wind! Ours are immortal.

BEATRICE
Fragile, and therefore beautiful. Gardens with blue flies and
yellow bees buzzing, grass where crickets and locusts sing. . . .
In our garden there are neither birds, nor insects nor lizards
sunning themselves on the fences, no chameleons, no doves . . .

RAPPACCINI
Enough, enough. You can't have everything. And our plants
are better. Their unpredictable shapes have the beauty of
febrile visions; their growth is steady like the slow advance of
a mysterious illness. Flowers and fruits as resplendent as jewels. But emeralds, diamonds and rubies are inert matter, dead
stones. Our jewels are alive. Fire passes through their veins
and changes color like the light in submarine caves. Garden
of fire, garden where life and death embrace and exchange
their secrets.

BEATRICE
True enough . . . but I would like to have a cat and stroke his
back until he becomes a sphere of perfume and electricity.
I'd like a chameleon to place on my skirt and watch it change
color. A cat, a chameleon, a yellow and green parrot that hops
on my shoulder shouting: Hey diddle, diddle, the cat and the
fiddle, the cow jumped over the moon. A little bird that I
can hide between my breasts. I'd like a . . .
Whimpering.

RAPPACCINI
Child, don't cry. I'm too sensitive and can't bear your suffering.

I would drink your tears.

BEATRICE
Angrily
You couldn't. They would burn you like acid.
To the tree.
Only you, brother, only you can receive my tears.
She embraces the tree.
Take my sorrow, drink in my life and give me a little of yours.
She picks a piece of fruit and eats it.
Forgive me; it's as if I were eating a piece of myself.
She laughs.

RAPPACCINI
Whew, I'm glad that's over.
He shrugs his shoulders and exits.

BEATRICE
To the tree.
I'm ashamed, brother. How can I complain? No other girl in
the city can walk through a garden like this, inhale the perfumes or eat the fruit that I eat. When I enter here, I feel as
if I were entering myself. The air envelops me like a vast im-
palpable body, the fragrance of the plants is warm as the smell
of a pure mouth, the moisture caresses me. It's there in the
house I suffocate, my head starts to pound, I get dizzy. If
you could walk you would sleep with me: your breath would
dissolve my bad dreams. If you could walk we could stroll
through the garden; if you could speak you would tell me
stories and we would laugh together.
She caresses the tree.
You would be tall and handsome. You would have white
teeth. The hair on your chest would be gold and thick as a
handful of herbs. Tall and serious. And there would be no
danger that you would love someone else: you couldn't. And
neither could I. No, I couldn't. I never will
To herself.
I am destined to go through this garden alone, talking to
myself.
To the tree.
Speak to me, tell me something; good afternoon.

42

JUAN
Appearing from the balcony.
Good afternoon!

BEATRICE
*Runs away, stifling a scream; then returns and
curtsies.*
Good afternoon!

JUAN
Throwing her the bouquet.
They're freshly cut roses! If you smell them they will tell
you my name.

BEATRICE
Thank you sir. My name is Beatrice.

JUAN
And I am Juan, I come from Naples and these roses . . .
BEATRICE *picks up the roses, clutches them to her
breast, starts to run and disappears, leaving* JUAN
speechless. The lights fade.

Scene IV

THE MESSENGER
The scene is in shadows; Juan's room is dimly lit.
Sleep, and while you sleep, battle against yourself. Has he
noticed that the bouquet of flowers turned black when Beatrice held them in her arms, as if struck by lightning? In the
uncertain twilight, with your head spinning from the exalta-
tions of the garden, it's not easy to distinguish a dry rose from
one freshly cut. Sleep, sleep! Dream of a sea the sun dresses
in purple and red streaks, dream of green hills, run along the
beach, return to your infancy! No, every moment you drift
farther away from familiar landscapes. You wander through
a city carved out of crystal. You thirst and the thirst gives
way to geometric deliriums. Lost in transparent corridors
you pass through circular plazas, passageways where melan-
choly obelisks guard fountains of mercury, streets that empty
into the same street. The walls of crystal enclose and imprison

you, your image is repeated a thousand times in another thousand mirrors. Condemned to remain within yourself, condemned to search for yourself in transparent galleries, always in sight, always unreachable: that which is there before you, that stares with pleading eyes and asks you for a signal, a sign of brotherhood and recognition, is not you, only your image. Condemned to sleep with your eyes open. Close them, go back, back to the darkness, beyond your infancy, farther back, to your origin! The waves of time pound against your soul! Row against them, row back, mount the current, close your eyes, fall into the seed. Someone has closed your eyelids. The transparent prison collapses, the walls of crystal lie at your feet, transformed into a pool of placid water. Drink without fear, sleep, navigate, let yourself be guided by the river of closed eyes. The morning is born at your side.

During his scene JUAN *mimes the Messenger's words.*

Scene V

ISABEL
Sir, Doctor Baglioni is here to see you.

JUAN
What, Doctor Baglioni, my father's friend?

ISABEL
The great doctor himself, sir, the honor of the university.

JUAN
Show him in, show him in! Or maybe it would be better if he waits; I'll dress and receive him in the parlor.

BAGLIONI
Entering
That won't be necessary, my young friend, your father was my roommate and study companion, in this very city. His son is my son.

Isabel bows and exits without speaking.

JUAN
Your visit embarrasses me, doctor. Please excuse the bare and

44

desolate room of a student. The circumstances . . .

BAGLIONI

I understand everything and I pardon everything. At last my
new friend is in Padua: the living image of his father. Sweet
memories are revived in this old heart, happy ones, sad ones,
all of them sacred!

JUAN

Your kindness is very moving, doctor. I'll tell you the reason
for my trip. I come to study law; I arrived yesterday and
couldn't find any lodging to suit my needs, other than this
bare room that you honor with your presence . . .

BAGLIONI

The view is lovely: there's a garden over on this side.

JUAN

And it's so unique. I've never seen anything like it. It belongs
to the famous Rappaccini.

BAGLIONI

Rappaccini?

JUAN

They say he is a scholar, the possessor of marvelous natural
secrets.

BAGLIONI

I see that you are well aware of our outstanding citizens,
whether legitimate or not. Actually, Rappaccini is a true man
of science. No one on the faculty is equal to him . . . with
only one exception.

JUAN

You know him, of course. With both of you living in the
same city and united by your mutual love of science, you
should be very good friends.

BAGLIONI

Slow down, my impetuous young man. Rappaccini loves
science, it's true; but the very violence of that love, or some
monstrous moral insensibility—I'm not sure which—has dark-
ened his soul. Men are like instruments to him, opportunities

for questionable experiments whose results, I should add, are almost always disastrous.

JUAN

He must be a dangerous man.

BAGLIONI

He is.

JUAN

Regardless, in whatever form, he does love science!

BAGLIONI

My son, science was made for man, not man for science.

JUAN

That doesn't prevent him from being the author of surprising discoveries.

BAGLIONI

At times he has been lucky. On the other hand, I know of occasions . . . But what interest do you have in your disturbing neighbor? You're not feeling ill, I hope?

JUAN

I've never felt better. Last night I left the door to the balcony open and slept like a log.

BAGLIONI

The air in Padua is very pure . . . As for Rappaccini . . .

JUAN

It's natural that since I just arrived in the city, his presence has aroused my curiosity. He is my neighbor. And they speak so much of his extraordinary love for science.

BAGLIONI

I hope they speak more of the results of this inhuman love.

JUAN
With a certain anger.
There is something on the earth more precious to Rappaccini than all of science, and for it he would sacrifice all his knowledge.

BAGLIONI

What?

JUAN

His daughter.

BAGLIONI

At last, my young friend, you have revealed your secret. So, the lovely Beatrice is the reason behind all this questioning!

JUAN

I have hardly spoken to her, only yesterday, in the afternoon.

BAGLIONI

No, don't apologize. I don't know this girl. I have heard it said that the young men of Padua are crazy about her . . . although they have hardly been introduced. They say that she is not only a beauty, but also a well of science, capable of occupying a chair on the faculty, despite her age.
He laughs.
Maybe mine. . . . But let's stop these idle rumors . . .
He directs Juan to the balcony.
Sad garden, profane monument to a blasphemous pride! It is said in Spanish: reason creates monsters.

JUAN

It may seem deplorable to us but we can't deny that his garden reveals a certain love, a kind of savage love for the truth, a passion for the infinite. That's why it makes your head spin . . .

BAGLIONI

Shhh! Rappaccini just stepped into the garden.
Rappaccini enters and examines his plants. Upon feeling himself observed he lifts his head and fixes his eyes on the balcony. BAGLIONI *gives him a cold greeting, which he doesn't respond to. For an instant, ignoring* BAGLIONI, *he intensely contemplates* JUAN. *He then exits.*

BAGLIONI

He saw us, although he didn't answer me. It's obvious his mind is on you. Have you met him?

JUAN
How could I, if I just got here?

BAGLIONI
I'm not sure, but I would swear he has an interest in you. A
scientific . . . interest. And what role does Beatrice play in
this conspiracy?

JUAN
Professor, don't you think you're carrying this a bit too far?
Neither the father nor the daughter is aware of my existence.

BAGLIONI
You can never be sure with Rappaccini. I'll think about what
I just saw. I wouldn't want anything to happen to the son of
an old friend.

JUAN
Sir, what are you trying to say?

BAGLIONI
For the moment, nothing. Hardly a suspicion . . . and yet a
certainty. But it must be getting late and they are expecting
me at the university. Will I have the pleasure of seeing you at
my home soon?

JUAN
I would be honored, Doctor Baglioni.

BAGLIONI
Good. Then, I'll be seeing you.
          He exits. JUAN *walks over to the balcony; before*
          he arrives, BAGLIONI *appears again.*

BAGLIONI
The nets that surround you are invisible, but they can strangle
you. If you help me, I can free you of them!
          He disappears.

Scene VI

JUAN *remains pensive; with a gesture he casts aside his thoughts; he walks toward the balcony; he withdraws; paces around the room; returns to the balcony; decided, he jumps down into the garden. He examines the plants with mistrust and curiosity. His movements suggest an intruder but at the same time are one of a man who shuns invisible dangers. He leans over a flower. At that moment* BEATRICE *appears in back of him.*

BEATRICE

Good morning! I see that our neighbor is also interested in flowers and plants.

JUAN

I don't know how to excuse my intrusion. I'm not a thief; the truth is that I'm fascinated by this strange vegetation; I couldn't resist the temptation and almost without thinking I jumped . . . and here I am!

BEATRICE

Don't apologize: I understand your curiosity and I'm sure my father will too. For him, curiosity is the mother of science.

JUAN

I wouldn't want to deceive you. Botany is not important to me, nor do the enigmas of nature keep me awake at night. I came to Padua to study law; chance has made us neighbors and yesterday I saw you—do you remember?—walking among these plants. It was then I discovered my true vocation.

BEATRICE

I'm sorry but I don't quite understand you. One look at the garden and you discovered your vocation? My father will be very proud . . .

JUAN

No, it's not the garden. When I saw you, among so much unknown foliage, I recognized it; it was life, familiar as a flower and, nevertheless remote. Life sprouting among the rocks in

49

the desert, with the same simplicity that the spring surprises us every year. All my being began to cover itself with green leaves. My head, instead of being this sad machine that produces confusing thoughts, changed into a lake whose only concern was to reflect the changes of the sky and the wholeness of the earth. Since then, I don't think: I reflect. Eyes opened or closed, I see nothing but your image.

BEATRICE

I am not familiar with the customs of the world; I have lived here alone since childhood and don't know how to respond. I also can't lie. And even if I could, I wouldn't. Your words have confused me but they haven't surprised me. I was expecting them, I knew you would have to say them, today or tomorrow.

JUAN

Beatrice!

BEATRICE

How beautiful my name is on your lips! No one has ever pronounced it that way.

JUAN

It's a bird; I say: Beatrice, and it spreads its wings and begins to fly, where I don't know. Away from here, to new heights. To follow it, to fly with you, nest in a cloud, live in a star, roam together on the beaches of the moon.

BEATRICE

When I saw you, it was as if the doors of my soul had opened. I was enclosed, surrounded by walls, blind. Suddenly a gust of wind opened the doors and windows. They made me want to jump and dance. That evening I felt I was flying. But I fell back into the garden. It seemed that the perfumes of all these plants had interwoven and formed a bodyless net of threads, that softly, with great tenderness, consumed me. I'm anchored to the earth. I am one of these plants. If I am picked, I will die. Go away, leave me here!

JUAN

Pushing away the imaginary net of perfumes with his hands.

I will open a path through this tissue of vapors; I will cut the enlaced branches of this invisible forest; with teeth and nails I will dig a tunnel through the wall. I will change into a sword and with one slash cut the curtain in two. I will untie the knot. I will show you the world. We will go south; the sea will rise up from its bed to greet you and shake its crest of salt; the green pines on my street will bow down to you . . .

BEATRICE
No, I don't know the world. The free air would imprison me.
She points to the garden
Its scent gives me life; if I glow it's because of its light. I am made of its substance. Stay here!

JUAN
To awaken to the light of your smile like a gulf that the dawn half opens, to be lulled asleep by the murmur of your blood that advances in waves through your body like a solar tide, to embrace you like a river around an island, breathe you, drink in the light that drinks up your mouth. You look at me and your eyes weave a dress of fire that doesn't burn, a fresh armor of golden ivy. Bathe in the clear water of your voice, pass endlessly through your body, sleep next to your breasts that are two new-born animals, dawn in your throat, die of thirst in front of your eyes, ascend the canal of your back and lose myself at the nape of your neck, travel down to your belly, navigate through your blood, every time deeper. Lose myself in you, the other shore, awaiting me. Be born in you, die in you.

BEATRICE
Spin incessantly around you, planet and sun.

JUAN
Face to face always, like two twin trees.

BEATRICE
Growing, sprouting leaves, flowers, ripening.

JUAN
Bind our roots.

BEATRICE
Enlace our branches.

JUAN
Confuse our fluids.

BEATRICE
One body.

JUAN
One tree, immense as the forest and tall as the sky.

BEATRICE
The stars nestle in our arms.

JUAN
The sun pauses to rest in our wine and sings.

BEATRICE
Its song is a fan that slowly opens and paints everything yellow.

JUAN
We are dressed in light.

BEATRICE
Made of the same invisible substance.

JUAN
We advance and the world opens at our footsteps.

BEATRICE
Waking up.
No, not that. The world begins and ends in you. And this
garden is our horizon.

JUAN
The world is infinite; it begins at your toe nails and ends at
the tips of your hair. You don't have an end.

BEATRICE
When I saw you, I also remembered. I remembered something
misplaced for some time but whose image was unerasable, like
a secret wound; something that came forth to tell me: look at
me, remember me, that which you have forgotten since birth,
is me.

52

JUAN
Staring at her.

I would like to open the wall of your forehead, lose myself in your thoughts and arrive at the center of your soul: who are you?

BEATRICE

You can read in my forehead everything you are thinking. It is a mirror that reflects you and never tires of repeating you. I am inhabited by your desire. Before you, I knew no one, not even myself. I didn't know there was a Sun, Moon, water, lips. I was one of these plants. I spoke often with this tree. It was the only friend I had. Yesterday you threw me some roses and they were like a bouquet of stars, a message from another world. What can I give you in return?

JUAN

Some flowers from this tree. Having them next to my pillow this evening will be like having you.
He approaches the tree and reaches out his hand to pick a flower.

BEATRICE

No, don't touch it! It would be fatal.
While she is speaking she touches Juan's hand. This has the force of an electric shock and she withdraws it quickly. BEATRICE *hides her head in her hands, terrified.* JUAN *attempts to approach her. She stops him with a gesture and runs toward the house.* JUAN *tries to follow her, but* RAPPACCINI *appears at the door.*

JUAN
Confused.
Excuse . . . me . . .

RAPPACCINI
Smiling.
Among neighbors there is no need to apologize.

JUAN

Without realizing it, attracted by these plants, I came into the garden. Its force was stronger than my will. And then I lingered too long . . . Maybe I should go.

RAPPACCINI

As you wish. But I must advise you that it will be difficult to leave the same way you came in. It will be better if I show you the door.

JUAN

Thank you, thank you.

RAPPACCINI

Making his way.

Over here.

They both exit; the lights fade.

Scene VII

The scene appears in a subdued light. In the background are JUAN *and* BEATRICE.

THE MESSENGER

Set apart from the world, the lovers wander among dubious flowers and inhale their equivocal scent, that stretches out like a crimson layer of delirium and then vanishes without leaving a trace, like the nocturnal images that melt into the waters of dawn. And in the same way, in the space of a few hours, five small blotches appear and disappear from Juan's right hand—the same one that Beatrice had touched the day before—five small red blotches, resembling five small flowers. But they don't question, or doubt, or even dream: they contemplate themselves, they breathe themselves. Do they breathe life or death? Neither Juan nor Beatrice think of life or death, of God or the Devil. They no longer care about saving their souls or obtaining riches or power, being happy or making others happy. It is enough to be face to face and look at each other. One encircling the other like two stars in love. He revolves around her and she spins around herself; the boundaries he describes are narrower each time; so she remains quiet and begins to enclose herself, petal by petal, like a nocturnal flower, until she becomes impenetrable. Undecided, he oscillates between desire and fear; finally he leans over her; powerless under his spell, she opens once again, unfolds, spins around her loved one and he remains still, fascinated. But they never touch, condemned to spin interminably, driven by two powerful enemies, that separate and unite them. Not a kiss or an embrace, just the eyes devouring the eyes in a battle that is an embrace. Surrounded by his gaze, she is a tower of fire and passion. If he touches her they will go up in flames.

While he is speaking, the couple mime the action of the words.

Scene VIII

The garden is empty. JUAN *and* BAGLIONI *are in the room.*

BAGLIONI
I hope I'm not interrupting anything. One of my patients lives near here, and I decided to drop by for a few minutes on my way to see him.

JUAN
Doctor, you will always be welcome here.

BAGLIONI
No, I don't have illusions. Older people always seem to bore the younger ones, we try to help but wind up irritating them instead. There's nothing you can do about it. That's life.
Pause.
I have been expecting you at the house.

JUAN
I assure you that my absence these past few days was not due to oversight but rather to . . . I spend the day studying . . .

BAGLIONI
Law, History, . . . Botany?

JUAN
Languages, Doctor, foreign languages.

BAGLIONI
Greek, Latin, Hebrew, the language of the birds . . .? But,

what a delicious perfume!

JUAN

Perfume?

BAGLIONI

Yes, a perfume, very faint but very powerful. It advances and retreats, appears and disappears, penetrates the depths of the lungs and dissolves in the blood like pure air . . .

JUAN

The imagination sometimes makes us see and even smell . . .

BAGLIONI

Interrupting.

No my son. This perfume is not a figment of my imagination but rather a reality of my senses. I'm serious: the aroma so suspiciously flooding your room. It comes from there, rises from that garden. It comes out of your mouth: you exhale it every time you open your lips. Rappaccini and his daughter, the astute Beatrice, administer death to their patients, surrounded by a cloak of lethal perfume!

JUAN

Say what you will about Rappaccini but don't mention Beatrice. Her mouth expels no poison, but only the purest words!

BAGLIONI

Rappaccini is a poisoner and his fatal mania has resulted in a despicable action: he has converted his daughter into a vial of venom!

JUAN

You're lying! Beatrice is innocent.

BAGLIONI

Innocent or guilty she transpires, exudes death.

JUAN

Beatrice is pure: her body has the firmness of stones, her skin the smoothness of fruit, her soul the transparency of water.

BAGLIONI

Accomplice or victim, it is the same. The truth is that Rappaccini has chosen you as the subject of a new and atrocious experiment. He is using his daughter as bait.

JUAN

Fantasies, fantasies, it's too horrible to be true.

BAGLIONI

And if it were?

JUAN

I would be lost! There would be no way out . . .

BAGLIONI

There is one. We'll trick Rappaccini. Listen.
He takes out a vial from his bag.
This vial contains an antidote more powerful than the bezoar stone, the stallion or the Roman cure. It is the fruit of many sleepless nights and years of study. If Beatrice is innocent, give it to her; in a short time she will recover her original nature. And now, good-bye. You hold your destiny in your hands.
JUAN wants to talk. BAGLIONI silences him with a finger, gives him the vial and exits.

Scene I X

JUAN

It's a fable, an invention of jealousy . . . But the bouquet of roses, the stains on my hand?
He looks at his hand.
No, there is nothing wrong with me. I enjoy splendid health. I am strong; I love life, life loves me. And if it were true . . .? How to find out . . .?
He walks around, indecisive. Suddenly he shouts.
Isabel, Madam Isabel! Come up right away, I need you.

VOICE OF ISABEL

Coming, coming!
While waiting for Isabel, JUAN looks in the mirror and touches himself.

ISABEL
What do you wish, sir?

JUAN
Nothing, a small favor: will you give me a rose? A rose like the one you brought me the day I arrived.

ISABEL
A rose?

JUAN
Yes, a red rose, a rose with drops of dew . . .

ISABEL
Bless my soul! The young man is in love.

JUAN
A freshly cut rose!

ISABEL
Right away, sir.
She exits.

JUAN
Even if Baglioni is right and Beatrice has been nurtured on poison, I am strong and sane. The air of Naples protects me . . . And if it all turns out to be a lie, I will cut out your tongue, Doctor Baglioni.

ISABEL
With the rose.
I didn't find any rose more beautiful than this one. Look at it: it's as if it were alive!

JUAN
Interrupting her.
Thank you, Madam Isabel.
He gives her a few coins.
And now leave me, I want to be alone.

ISABEL
Holy Virgin, what whims! The young!
She exits.

JUAN
With the rose in his hand.
A red rose, a small quivering heart, a small radiant sun between
my hands. A thirsty rose.
He blows on it.
Refresh yourself, breathe in life.
*The rose turns black; horrified he lets it drop to the
floor.*
It's true, it's true! My breath kills, I carry death in my blood!
I am damned, cut off from life! I am separated from the
world by a wall of poison which binds me to a monster.

BEATRICE
From the garden.
Juan, Juan! The sun is high and the plants are calling us.

JUAN
He ponders, and then decides.
Wait, I'll jump down and be there in a second.
He jumps.

BEATRICE
Since dawn I have counted the hours until we could be together. The garden doesn't seem mine without you. You are
like a tree that has been here since my childhood: the biggest,
the strongest, the most resplendent. In my dreams I speak to
you but you don't answer: you speak the language of a tree,
and instead of saying words you give fruit.

JUAN
Impatiently
What kind of fruit?

BEATRICE
Great golden fruit, the fruit of dreams. Didn't I tell you that
I dreamt it.
Looking at a plant.
Look, it changed color. And how it smells. Its aroma puts the
garden to sleep.

JUAN
Angrily.
It must be a very strong narcotic.

BEATRICE
With simplicity.
I don't know. I'm not familiar with many of the properties
of the plants. And my father doesn't know all their secrets
either, although he says he does. Of course, they are new.

JUAN
New? What do you mean?

BEATRICE
What a question! You don't know? These plants never existed before, they are species invented by my father. He cor-
rects nature, he adds richness, as if giving life to life.

JUAN
I'd say that he enriches death. This garden is an arsenal.
Every leaf, every flower, every root, is a mortal weapon, an
instrument of torture. We pass quietly through the house of
the executioner and we are moved before his creations . . .

BEATRICE
Stop! It's horrible what you are saying.

JUAN
Is there something more horrible than this garden? Something more horrible than ourselves? Listen to me, poor Beatrice, do you realize who you are and how you live? The
plague, typhoid, leprosy, the mysterious diseases that cover
the body with a jewelry of scarlet sores, the vines of fever, the
spiders of delirium, the eyes that explode and corrupt noon,
green slime . . . all of it is condensed here. This garden is a
tumor on the innocent heart of the city . . .

BEATRICE
Listen to me! You can't condemn me without letting me
speak . . .

JUAN
Stand back, don't touch me! Incarnation of the plague, rotten apple, poisoned apple. Death, and adorned with the most
sacred attributes of life!

60

BEATRICE

Your words are vicious and they burn me. But they are just and purify me.

JUAN

Do you dare to speak of purity, you who corrupt the world with your breath? You were alone, an abandoned island. You chose me. Now you have an accomplice; you can rejoice: together, our breath will dry up the harvest and poison the fountains.

Pause.

Speak, say something!

BEATRICE

Calmly.

I was expecting this. I knew everything you were going to say. But I was crazy and put my trust in a miracle. I have lived alone since childhood content with my fate. At times, the murmur of the world would pound against the walls of this house like an enticing wave; and those calls troubled me: my blood throbbed with another beat, my dreams were peopled with unknown images. Then, when I looked at the garden, intoxicated by its fatal aroma, I forgot that there were cats, roses, horses, carnations, men. What could apples, pomegranates, pears, matter to me if I had the fruits of this tree, that was like the tree of Paradise? My father would say to me: within this tree, death has become life.

JUAN

It's ridiculous. What you call life begets sickness, madness, death. Your breath kills.

BEATRICE

My breath kills, not my thoughts. I belong to my father, to his infinite dream. Like these plants, I was a replica and a challenge to nature: the most powerful poisons circulate in my veins, harmlessly. I was one of the creations of my father: the most daring, the most rash, the most . . .

JUAN

Doomed.

BEATRICE

Doomed.

JUAN

The most guilty . . .

BEATRICE

It's not my fault. Nothing living surrounded me, I did no harm to anyone, except myself. I never had a cat, a dog, or a canary. No one taught me how to sing, no one played with me, no one trembled with me in a dark room. My life was growing, breathing, ripening, ahh, ripening!

JUAN

With tenderness and hate.
Ripening like an exquisite fruit, infinitely desirable, infinitely untouchable.

BEATRICE

I lived the life of a seed, alone, drawn into myself, planted in the center of my being. Isolated.

JUAN

Island that will never have one human footprint, island away from the greatest routes, alone, forever alone, lost in the immensity of time, condemned to never leave yourself.

BEATRICE

Asleep, without memories or desires, well-anchored to the earth, well-planted in myself. Then the world split in two. You picked me like a plant, cut my roots, threw me into the air. Suspended in your eyes, I tight-roped through the void. Now I am nowhere. I could throw myself at your feet but I won't: I would poison your shadow.

JUAN

Condemned to gaze at each other without ever touching. Condemned to remain within ourselves.

BEATRICE

It's enough to look at you. Your gaze is enough. I am not my own person. I don't have my own existence, my own soul, my own body. Your thought invaded me, there was no cave or hiding place that you didn't penetrate. There is no room in me for myself. But I don't want to be in me, but in you. Let me be one of your thoughts, the least significant! And then, forget me.

RAPPACCINI

Invisible, lost in the garden: only his voice is heard.
My child, you are no longer condemned to solitude. Pick one of the flowers off our tree and give it to your beloved. He can touch it without fear. And he can touch you. Thanks to my science—and to the secret congeniality of the blood—your natural opposites have been reconciled. The two can now be one. Bound together you will pass through the world, feared by all, invincible, like gods.

JUAN

Surrounded by hate, surrounded by death. Like two snakes hidden in the cracks of the earth.

VOICE OF RAPPACCINI

Stupid! Surrounded by amazement and reverent fear, conquerors of life, impenetrable, magnificent donors of death.

JUAN

You're crazy but your pride will never destroy us, we will not fall into your trap! There is a way out, a bridge. I have the key to our freedom. Beatrice, take this antidote and drink it without fear: you will recover your true nature.
He gives her the vial.

VOICE OF RAPPACCINI

No, don't drink it my child, don't drink it. The antidote will be poison for you. You will die.

JUAN

Drink it, it's another of the old man's tricks. Drink it without fear and renounce this monster. You will be free.

VOICE OF RAPPACCINI

You ignorant fool! The elements of her blood have assimilated my poison in every conceivable way. Any antidote would mean instant death. My child, don't drink it!

BEATRICE

Father, if you condemned me to solitude why didn't you tear
out my eyes? Then I wouldn't have seen him. Why didn't
you make me deaf and dumb? Why didn't you plant me in
the earth like this tree? Then I wouldn't have run after his
shadow . . .

To JUAN.

Ahh, blind, deaf, dumb, tied to the ground with irons I would
have run to you. My thoughts embrace your image like ivy; I
am bound to the wall with thorns and claws, I tear myself
away and fall at your feet.

JUAN

Oh Beatrice, all the doors have been closed!

BEATRICE

The doors were closed. You arrived and the door of love
opened. But then you withdrew. Everything is closed again.

JUAN

I opened my eyes and saw myself planted in this garden, like
a forsaken tree, cut off from the flow of life.

BEATRICE

To arrive there, to true life, we walked under the arches of
death with closed eyes. But you opened yours, you weak-
ened . . .

JUAN

I was dizzy! Open your eyes, look at me, look at life!

BEATRICE

No, I am returning to myself. At last I am passing through
myself and I possess myself. I wander in darkness, I penetrate
my being, sink to my roots and touch the place of my birth.
Statue, blood without exit, island, solitary rock, tower of
flames: I begin and end in myself. I am surrounded by a river
of knives, untouchable.

VOICE OF RAPPACCINI

Listen to me crying I beg of you: don't drink it. I will give
you a way back, I will compel nature to change her course. I
wanted you to be stronger than life: now I will humiliate death.

64

BEATRICE
Drinking.
I have made the final leap, and now I am on the other shore.
Garden of my infancy, poisoned paradise, tree, my brother,
my son, my only lover, my only husband, cover me, embrace
me, burn me, dissolve my bones, dissolve my memory! I am
falling, I am falling inside myself and still not touching the
bottom of my soul!

RAPPACCINI
Appearing.
My child, why have you abandoned me!

Epilogue

THE MESSENGER
One after the other parade the figures—The Juggler, the Hermit, the Lady—one after the other they appear and disappear,
come together and separate. Guided by the stars as by the
will without the language of the blood, they march on, always farther, to the encounter of themselves; they intersect
and merge for an instant and then disperse and lose themselves in time. Like the planned movement of the suns and
planets, they untiringly repeat the dance, condemned to
search, condemned to find themselves, lose themselves, and
search for themselves without rest through infinite corridors.
Peace to those who search, peace to those who are alone and
spin in the void. Because yesterday and tomorrow don't exist:
everything is today, everything is here, present. What passed,
is still passing.

trans. by Harry Haskell

☆　　　　☆　　　　☆

65

Octavio Paz

MOVEMENT

If you are the mare of amber
       I am the path of blood
If you are the first falling snow
       I am the dawn's brazier lighter
If you are the tower of night
       I am the nail searing your brow
If you are the morning tide
       I am the cry of the first bird
If you are the orange basket
       I am the knife cast of sunlight
If you are the altar of stone
       I am the hand that defiles it
If you are the earth in repose
       I am the unripe sugarcane
If you are the leap of the wind
       I am the fire deeply buried
If you are the mouth of the sea
       I am the mouth of the boglands
If you are the forest of clouds
       I am the hatchet that cleaves them
If you are the city profaned
       I am the hallowing rainfall
If you are the yellow mountain
       I am the red arms of algae
If you are the sun arising
       I am the path of blood

from Salamandra
trans. by Robert Lima

Octavio Paz

CUSTODIA

The name
Its shadings
The male   The female
The mallet   The gong
The i   The o
The tower   The cistern
The index   The hour
The bone   The rose
The dew   The tomb
The spring   The flame
The brand   The night
The river   The city
The keel   The anchor
The he-she   The she-male
Humankind
Its body of names
Your name in my name In your name my name
One facing the other one against the other one around the other
The one in the other
without names

from Ladera este
trans. by Robert Lima

Octavio Paz

HIMACHAL PRADESH (2)

Ours
>   (shaved head, paunchy and)
is the mooost ancient
>   (greasy)
Civilization in the
>   (on the goat path
>   his saffron robe was a flame)
>   *World!*
(in motion)
>   *This land is*
(and the murmur of his sandals
on the dry pine needles)
>   *Holy:*
the land of
>   (was as if he stepped on) *the Vedas.*
(ashes.)
>   *Man*
>   (With his forefinger)
began to think
>   (categorically)
>   *five thousand years ago*
(the pundit pointed out)
>   *Here* . . .
>   (the Himalayas,
the youngest mountains on this planet).

from Ladera este
trans. by Robert Lima

68

José L. Varela-Ibarra

NOTES ON THE "NOCTURNE OF SAN ILDEFONSO" BY OCTAVIO PAZ

1

Both external and internal space are creations of the mind.
On an invented space we plant our signs/seeds. What is La
Plaza del Zocalo, what is Mexico, what is the San Ildefonso
school, if not mental pictures?

2

San Ildefonso is the preparatory school in Mexico City where
Octavio Paz studied as a youngster. But the space in the poem
has slight ties with urban geography. The space in this poem
is a visionary space. The Poet's eyes are closed from the beginning. Space is created by his mind, the imagining side of
the mind, and it is a perceptual space and a magical space.
It illuminates and transforms reality, making it more real.

3

The poem begins at the window. There outer and inner space
are joined. The sensation produced is at the same time one
of a larger space and of a more reduced space. The window
is the bridge between here and there, now and then, inside
and outside, sanity and insanity. Perhaps all poems are windows: our effort and desire to unite contraries.

4

The window takes us from inner to outer space and back
again to inner space. Back again: in Spanish, *de vuelta*. The
title of the book in which the poem appears: *Vuelta*.

5

The space of the window is the space of silence. The window
does not speak. Noises come from out there. The only human
voice we hear is that of the Poet, in a monologue full of anger
and disillusionment.

6

Octavio Paz returns to Mexico after years abroad (ambassador
to India, etc.). He returns not only to the physical space, that
invention we call Mexico City, but to the mental space:
Memory. It is not that such and such a street or building
remind him of something. He is returning to something he
left at such and such a street or building. Octavio Paz finds
spaces that recognize him and some that don't.

7

When we think about the past, especially about our ideals in
the past, we feel disillusioned. But when we realize that the
past and present are the same, we feel anger.

8

The adjectives in the poem contribute not only to the tone
of anger, but also to describe us. Isolate the adjectives and
see if they don't apply to you and me.

9

Translations will never convey the full semantic import of a
word: the reverberations a single word has in the mental space
of a reader. La Plaza del Zocalo is a huge square in Mexico
City. Around it are the Cathedral and important government
offices, the National Palace, etc. When Octavio Paz writes in
Spanish: "La Plaza del Zocalo: vasta como firmamento . . ."
we can translate it literally as: "The Zocalo Square: huge as
the heavens." But phonetically "vasta" (huge) and "basta"
(enough) are the same. "Firmamento" may mean heavens and
also the place where stars, including political stars, live. The
line can be received as: Zocalo Square: enough of this
government!

10

Thirteen of the twenty poems in the book *Vuelta* make use
of the verb "caer" (to fall). The movement of the "Nocturne"
is vertical. The Poet goes to the window and jumps. (Octavio
Paz does live in a sixth floor penthouse.) He falls to the city,
then to the page where the poem appears. The page is a significant space in Paz's poetry. Falling can take us to Jung.

(MLA professors can now run to their next convention with
a paper on "Jungian Motifs in the Poetry of Octavio Paz.")

11

The "Nocturne" is the temporalization and spacialization of
the Poet's internal visions. Now he is no longer the prisoner
of his sixth floor cage. The two paths of Octavio Paz: love
and poetry. He can depend on the love of his wife (see how
the poem ends) and on poetry. (Religion? "I am not interested
in religion," he told me a few months back when I visited him.)

12

The poem ends with the Poet, eyes closed, listening to the
waves of his breath. This is meditation, if not "religion."
The Poet is awake. And is this not our purpose, to awaken
to life? What does he hear? Breathing. Nothing else. When
he speaks, no one answers him. He lives in a world that is
part of a brotherhood over the void. The rest: heaven/hell
of the business world, a loneliness he shares with his wife,
who sleeps, and with silence.

☆   ☆   ☆

Edwin Honig

A CONVERSATION WITH OCTAVIO PAZ

The following conversation took place on October 16, 1975, between Octavio Paz and Edwin Honig.

Edwin Honig: As I was saying to you, Octavio, I feel a certain constraint to limit this discussion so as not to repeat matters you have already explained in print, except when they are interestingly problematical. To begin, I'd like to ask about your own first experiences as a translator. How did you decide that you must be a translator?

Octavio Paz: I didn't decide really. It was, well, as always, an accident. But also, as always, when we talk about accidents, we also talk about desire. When I came to the United States the first time, I said, "I must learn English better, because I want to read American and English poets." So I learned English mainly to read poetry. Then, reading English and French poems, I felt that they should be known in Spanish. You see, it was desire, love—and with love, the desire for participation.

Honig: When you became interested in translation, had the chief English and American poets been translated—like Eliot and Pound?

Paz: Eliot, yes, but not Pound. Until recently he was not very well known in Spanish-speaking countries. Eliot was widely and, sometimes, very well translated. I remember one of my first encounters with modern poetry. I was studying for my college preparatory examinations, and at that time, around 1931, there was in Mexico a good literary magazine, *Contemporaneos*. It was published by a group of older poets. In one issue, featuring modern poetry, there were poems by Neruda, Borges, Alberti, Guillén, all of them not very well known in those years. I was struck by two translations: *The Waste Land* and *Anabase*. Eliot and Perse, both in the same issue!

Honig: When you started to translate from another language, did you have a feeling during part of your working that you

72

wanted to be the poet you were translating?

Paz: Well, no, I don't think so.

Honig: So, your experience as a translator extends over a number of years. You still translate?

Paz: Well, sometimes, yes. When I like some poems. Or when I have been asked, or because I am a friend of the poet's. One of the main reasons for translating is a moral urge, a didactic impulse. I think that Pound translated many things—Chinese poetry, for instance, *The Confucian Anthology*—for didactic purposes.

Honig: Yes, it was part of what he called the *paideia*—the course of reading which every civilized English reader would need to follow (as this is presented, for instance, in *The ABC of Reading*), something he thought a lot about.

I have recently reread your essay on translation which appeared in *TLS* a few years ago and want to ask about the two or three main subjects you bring in. You speak of the text as the subject of translation. And I have thought of the text as often being a variable quantity and quality. The famous phrase of Robert Frost's—poetry is "what gets lost in translation"—doesn't cover the situation. If something is lost, something is also recovered. The feeling of what gets recovered or found isn't mentioned much. But is there anything that is stable in terms of the text?

Paz: I should say that poetry is what gets transformed. After all, poetry is not merely the text. The text produced the poem: a set of sensations and meanings. Now, what is the text? The text is signs—these signs can be written or oral, and they produce meanings. Signs are material things; you can see or hear them. Signs are things which produce meanings, but meanings are not things. In prose the function of the signs is, mainly, to produce meanings; in poetry, the material properties of the signs, especially the sound, are also essential. In poetry you cannot separate the sign from the meaning. Poetry is the marriage of the sensual or physical half of language with its ideal or mental half. Poetry is "impossible" to translate because you have to reproduce the materiality of the signs, its physical properties. Here is where translation as an *art* begins: since you cannot use the same signs of the original, you must find equivalents. The text is lost, but its effects can be reproduced through other signs; with different means, you can produce similar results. I say *similar,* not *identical.* Translation is an art of analogy, the art of finding correspondences. An art of shadows and echoes. What we have called transformation can be called analogy also. Translation is the art of producing, with different means, analogous effects. I think Valéry said something like that. Or, we can put it in a more radical way: translation is the art of producing, with a different text, a poem similar to the original. I will give you two examples of the transformation of the text. Pierre Leiris, the French translator of Eliot, *with his approbation,* rendered "In the room the women come and go/Talking of Michelangelo" as *"Dans le salon les femmes vont et viennent/en parlant des maitres de Sienne."* He tried to reproduce the *effect* and he had to change the text. Translating a sonnet by Mallarmé— the famous sonnet *IX*—I had to face a most difficult line: *"aboli bibelot d'inanite sonore."* He is speaking of a seashell (a *"ptyx")* lying on a table or sideboard. I wanted to produce a similar effect by different means: *"Espiral espirada de inanidad sonora."* The idea of "bibelot" was slightly displaced, without disappearing, and I underlined that form of the seashell *(espiral).* But I preserved the idea of extinction *(aboli, espirada)* and the play of sounds *(bibelot, espiral).*

Honig: Let's go back to the question of the text, or as I would prefer to put it regarding translation, "the absent text." At any rate, the idea of "the absent text"—the text that is not there—seems to point to a more useful way of thinking about what happens in translation. Of course it's true that a good deal of the poetry that we know about comes through the ear and not the eye. It is aural/oral. And there's a tremendous renaissance of interest going on right now in oral poetry.

Paz: Yes, I'm distressed when I *hear* the French critics speaking all the time about "writing"—*l'ecriture.* I think that they are missing something very important. Poetry has always been *spoken.* Speech is something you hear, not something you read.

Honig: So from the oral point of view, we see what otherwise has been latterly so hard to understand—as you put it, the false idea that a literal translation is the only true or possible one.

Paz: The literal is not a translation. Even in prose. Only mathematics and logic can be translated in a literal sense. Real prose—fiction, history—has rhythms and many physical properties, like poetry. When we translate it, we accomplish the same as we do with poems: transformations, metaphors.

Honig: The term in Spanish for literal—what you call *servil*—suggests where the emphasis really belongs. Literal translation, if possible at all, does not make for an interesting literary effect.

Paz: You know, perhaps we should say that there are three kinds of translation. One is literal translation, which is conceivable and useful in learning a language. Then you have the literary translation, where the original is changed in order to be more "faithful" and less "literal." And then you have another kind, imitation, which is neither literal nor faithful. The point of departure in imitation is the same as that of the literary translation: the original poem. Its point of arrival is different: another poem.

Honig: Each type is meant to serve a different purpose—a kind of special use—and to have a certain effect. Now if it's true that most of the history of culture and literature involves poetry as an oral matter, without a written text (and of course there are still poets who hate to type a poem or write it down, and would much prefer to speak it), one sees that the creative act is a re-creative act at the same time. Each "oral poet" (like the Homeric bard) is engaged in re-saying the same poem in different ways.

Paz: The creative act is made up of tradition and invention. To make a poem you have to have certain patterns like meter and, in many cases, rhyme also. Then, figures of speech. All these are given, handed to you by your tradition. At the same time you must say something new, personal. So that when you write a poem you are inventing something, but you are also repeating something very old. When you invent too much, it's a disaster, because then you have a text which cannot be communicated. When you don't invent at all, it's a disaster, because then you have a text which is not interesting enough to communicate. It must be balanced. That same thing happens when you translate. Translation is only one degree of this balance between repetition and invention, tradition and creation. Perhaps we should say more: each original poem is the translation of the unknown or absent text.

Honig: There may be another way to put this. Somewhere I read (and it's documented in a recent book by George Steiner) that the Cabala states that in the beginning God's word was lost or broken up—i.e., that there existed an original, universal language as well as a word which summed up everything. From this point of view, it may be said that what the translation does and what the original tried to do are both attempts to rewrite, reform, and bring together some of the broken pieces of that letter. The attempt to recover a lost or absent text that once existed is at the basis of translation. But, also, both the original and the translation are simply two attempts to do the same thing.

Paz: You are right. The idea that the world is a broken text is a variation—a frightful one—of the idea of the universe as a book. This image was popular in the Middle Ages and through the Renaissance. It was taken up by the Romantics and the Symbolists. Baudelaire says that poetry is essentially analogy. The idea of universal correspondence comes from the idea that language is a microcosmos, a double of the universe. Between the language of the universe and the universe of language, there is a bridge, a link—poetry. The poet, says Baudelaire, is the translator—the universal translator and the translator of the universe. This idea of poetry as translation is related to the Cabalistic idea.

Everything was *signed* or put into signs in the sixteenth and seventeenth centuries. Everything could be reduced to an emblem—a signature. Dante at the end of the *Commedia* sees God, the Trinity, the mystery we can *see* but can't talk about, and he sees it is a kind of book . . . with loose, floating pages. For the Greeks the idea of the word was central. Also for the Hebrews. In the case of our Hebrew-Christian civilization, there is this idea of the Book.

Honig: Roualt says in *Reflections sur l'art* that man, if you think of him in everything he does, is really collecting words and pasting them up somewhere. You see signs everywhere; you see books and papers. You see the hunger and the frantic pursuit of information as an almost universal activity. Almost everyone is engaged in putting letters on paper, in reading things, making out signs. And if you'd come to earth from another planet, you would say these people are crazed by the idea of letters.

Paz: I don't know if you have read *Logique du vivant* by the French geneticist Jacob. He explains that the whole genetic program of cells can be reduced to a single command: duplicate. In order to achieve this self-replicating aim, they must die. In the program of the cells—I should say, the program of life—is written the word *death*. The keyword of the message in all living organisms is death. Duplication and death. This message is spoken in thousands of ways, and it is carried on by all creatures. That is universal translation.

The universe speaks. And it says: die—and duplicate. All living forms are versions and translations of this phrase. Cells, stars, atoms—everything is saying the same thing in a different language. Here you see the universe as a book but as a book which has only one sentence and millions of translations of that single sentence. Not all are faithful—there are accidents, mutations, variants. And it has one exception: man. Because he refuses to die and doesn't want to duplicate.

Honig: Why do we refuse to die?

Paz: Each man feels himself unique, singular. Each man believes that *he* is as no one else. He *is* an ego, a soul. The souls are the opposite of cells. They are unique, and they don't duplicate. Man refuses death, the self-replicating program of the cells, and tries to save his unique soul in different ways, from work to art and from religion to science. He does not want self-duplication but preservation or, if you like, self-perpetuation.

Honig: What does man want to preserve that is so important to life?

Paz: Cells want to duplicate because they don't have an ego; they are soulless. Man wants to save his soul or his ego, not

77

his life. From the ego spring the two ideas that have ob-
sessed us: that we are unique and that this uniqueness must
be preserved in some way. This way is not duplication but
transformation. Duplication is literal translation. Exact identity between the original and the copy. Transformation is
poetic or literary translation. Man translates the universe and
by translating it changes it. This applies to Baudelaire and to
the Cabala but also to science and culture. It applies to civilization. Think of the Chinese translating the Sanskrit texts,
or the Jews translating in Alexandria the Bible in Greek, and
the Romans translating the Greeks. The history of the different civilizations is the history of their translations. Each civilization, as each soul, is different, unique. Translation is our
way to face this otherness of the universe and history.

Honig: Is it known about the Aztecs or the Incas, whether
they translated?

Paz: They translated; they took things from other civilizations;
and what they took they changed. If you think that translation is not only a verbal phenomenon, then you can accept
history as translation. In this sense, they did translate. And
also in the verbal sense: pre-Columbian Mexico was a polyglot
society. The Conquest can be seen as an extraordinary exercise in translation. As you know, Cortez had as interpreter a
famous and intelligent Indian woman who became his mistress,
Malinche or Doña Marina. She knew Nahuatl and Maya, and
at the beginning of her relation with Cortez they had to use
another interpreter, the Spaniard Aguilar, a former prisoner
of the Mayans who knew this language and Spanish. From
Nahuatl (Malinche) to Maya (Aguilar) to Spanish (Cortez).

Honig: An amazing set up, presenting itself at a time when it
was most needed. Now, I wonder if there's such a thing as a
source, or original, civilization. We speak, for example, of an
Indo-European language, assuming an original though quite
hypothetical language of that description.

Paz: You mean that there may have been one original language?
I don't know, and even if it could have been, I don't think
knowledge of the fact would have an important bearing for
our purpose. I believe that there has always been, from the
beginning, a plurality of texts. You were talking about the

absent text—the "idea" or archetype of the text. In reality there is not a single text; there is always an *"ur-text"*—the never written and never spoken "original," always virtual and always appearing in many versions, all saying the same thing and saying different things. And that is the paradox of literature, I think, and of art: the great works say the same thing, and at the same time say it differently.

Honig: Now let me ask—when does any translation stay put? When does a translation stabilize itself? That is, one is aware of the activity of languages changing all the time, so that the language of the last generation is not our language. But there are certain works that persist, no matter how much the language changes. The *King James Bible,* or, if you regard Shakespeare as a good translator of Plutarch, which he is, *that* stays put, whatever it is he has transmuted.

Paz: Well, Shakespeare is one moment of the text, a kind of pivotal figure of the processes to follow.

Honig: Now, this is also related: certain translations continue to be fresh and marvelous, even in an antiquated form of the language. The vigorous sixteenth-century translation of the *Celestina,* for example, by Thomas Mabbe, the Englishman, is still a joy to read. Against the rule that there need to be new translations every generation, this is a rare phenomenon. Of course there is such a thing as a sacred book, as Homer was in a religious sense once, and as Shakespeare is now, a book sacred to our culture, you might say. In fact what we regard as classics in art and literature are moments of sacred artistic accomplishments.

Paz: And those books are the most widely translated.

You know, I'd also like to talk about the practice as well as the theory of translation. We start with love. You *must* love the text. Then, you must know your own language, and also you must have a good knowledge of the text you are translating. You must work very hard, have very good dictionaries, a good technique, and finally inspiration. Inspiration is something that comes not from the stars but from inside, from working. Inspiration is linked with work and is linked with the dictionary. Without the dictionary you don't have inspiration.

Honig: A dictionary—that's another book!

Paz: It's the book as the universe, again. It is the sentence, but the broken sentence. The dictionary is the real double of the universe—only it is broken, disjointed. With the dictionary you can make all the books, but which would be the Real One?

Honig: There's one other aspect to this, the relation between translation and creation. You experimented in such a way with the *renga,* the versions of poems in four languages by four different poets—a very interesting way of re-creating poetry. It brings together the translation, and the original in one act.

Paz: Yes, it's true. *That* is the thing: the transformation, the changed text, coming from a text in English, then one in French, one in Spanish, then Italian. All these transformations are a creative and not simply a mechanistic process.

Honig: This interests me as a psychological use of game-playing with language. In a way, it's a joke, but also a sort of "controlled experiment" of four different-language poets who pretend to be subjects of some kind of master idea, to which they are bound to respond. You explained it as taking place in a hotel basement in Paris overnight. Can you say something about the *renga* game?

Paz: You can also say it's an experiment in the sense that we were trying to be both the objects and the observers. It could also be called collective writing. And a ceremony or a game— all this together. A game, because it was subject to rules and was a gratuitous activity; a rite because we were doing something very old: trying to reactualize a Japanese practice of a poetry commune. And then, the idea behind that was that we were only the instruments of *another* author. This author was language itself—the language which was also changing as we wrote, changing with the tongue of each poet. It could be summed up as game, experiment, joke, rite, mystification, ceremony. When you are writing your own poem you are doing the same thing. It is a game and a ceremony—don't you think? A rite.

Honig: What did you feel about the poems that came out of it?

Paz: Well, I think I should not say anything about the poems. I'm one of the authors.

Honig: I don't blame you.

Paz: I believe the primary thing was the activity. I was thinking of doing it again, but in only one language.

Honig: Well, that too would be interesting. There is, of course, a game of that sort that's well known. Someone creates the first line, and then mails it to someone else in another city who adds another line, and so on. It's called a chain letter.

Paz: The surrealists played a similar game, and it was called "the exquisite corpse."

Honig: Something both primitive and sophisticated.

Paz: Speaking of the *renga*, you know the surrealists were very addicted to spontaneity, the unconscious, and chance. And in this sense our *renga* was not surrealist. It was chance but controlled. It was accident but also according to rules. Only in a work done according to the rules can you have accidents.

Honig: But did you feel that while you were engaged in this collaborative poem, the rite and experimenting with the languages, that you were also repeating an experience that was normal and very old, going back to what is called primitive society?

Paz: The *renga* is not that ancient. It was done in the fourteenth century.

Honig: I was thinking of the activity of the shamans.

Paz: Yes, there is a relationship. *Renga* is only one form of the old and universal practice of collective poetry. We can say that poetry is always collective because you always have a reader or a listener. Always, at least, two: the text, the voice —and that listener. But I have read that there's a tribe on the frontier of Bolivia and Paraguay. They're nomads. And this people, who are very few, hunt all day. They make camp at night, and, after the meal, the men go to face the night, on each of the four different parts of the horizon. And there they invent poems that they say to the spirits of the night. It is all about their prowess in hunting, a kind of epic poetry that the hunter makes for nobody but the night and its spirits.

Is that not moving? That could be the negation of translation. That could be the great exception.

When you're reading a poem you're translating, when you're reading Shakespeare, you're doing a translation—translating him into the American sensibility in the twentieth century. But the poem of the hunter would never be heard and translated; it's all meant to be between him and the night only.

Honig: Isn't that where it begins, between a man and some voice that calls him, and he has to answer? I remember when I was a boy reading the Old Testament in Hebrew and being very awed by . . .

Paz: You can read Hebrew?

Honig: I did then. I can make it out now. When God said, *Vayoimar Adonai al Mosche,* "and God said to Moses, Come," and Moses said, "I am here," *(Hinani,* I am here). And I think of that connection as a sort of formula, presenting a very dramatic moment. When God called man and he said, I am here, it established a conjunction. So that whatever was said, as God told him to do this and that, was said only between the two of them. Later, when Moses went up on the mountain and he was alone there, for however long he was there, it was a very terrible moment, because maybe it was like that moment you just described with the Indians in the night. The moment of being alone with the creation and one's creation.

Paz: With our soul. When the hunter talks with the night and the spirits, he talks to himself. The reader, the listener is— yourself. Many times as a boy I used to hike in Mexico, when we had a beautiful valley, which isn't so now, since it has become polluted. But then it was very beautiful to walk through, and sometimes you cried out, and you heard the echo, and that's all. Our great solitude in nature.

Honig: The last syllable of the word. You're talking about the last syllable—"the last syllable of recorded time."

☆　　　　　☆　　　　　☆

Claude Esteban

POETRY AS INSURRECTION

On the verge of each poem by Octavio Paz, in the first breath which gives birth to it, there is less the desire for an affirmation than the sudden awakening, as in the morning—the individual, mind and body, in an almost uncontrollable flight towards what is undefined, outside; towards what has neither place nor form nor figure; and will gain all this from a man and from his glance. What claims our attention, even beyond the magnificence of a word—from the first lines of *Luna silvestre* to the feverish overture of "Petrificada petrificante," written some forty years later—is this refusal of the inevitable, this rebellion incited without end against the certainties already gained—yesterday's knowledge—and facing that knowledge, the dark wall, as if unbroached, of the world.

> I open my eyes
> > I am
> Still alive
> > At the center
> Of a wound still fresh

Others—and so near us—have invested the poetic enterprise with the value only of "restricted action," abandoning the world of the senses to its enigmas, to its wanderings, in order to save in the end, the joy of a few words set side by side. Octavio Paz has not heard these invitations—or, fervent reader of Mallarmé, he has not believed that the destiny of modern poetry should be wholly identified with the dark descent towards the tomb of Midnight in which Igitur's will was buried, and with his will the ambition of a word which could sustain Being. Isn't it still the poet's task to fight off the menacing hegemony of Signs, to keep the distance from growing too great between the vocables that summon reality and the little reality which remains to us? . . . It is true that the gods have left; that our symbols have grown old; that things have lost their native force, their substance; and those who question them, with their gestures, their words, have lost the power to restore their weight, their place, their presence at the heart of a universe which slips through their hands and where they themselves are at a loss for a footing. This ontological failure, pushed at times to the edge of the intolerable, is the only foundation on which Octavio Paz will build those "wandering republics of sound and meaning" which constitute his poems.

I believe that much more is at stake than the anxiety of a writer who might judge himself to be of secondary importance, and perhaps superfluous, faced with the unmistakable immediacy of phenomena, and the experience of action. In his memorable letter to Léon Felipe, Octavio Paz does not hide from himself that "To write poetry is / Learning to read / The empty space of writing." But this cavity our signs are drawn into as soon as they are spoken or stabilized, this vertigo of vanity is not merely self-referential. No, it is not only language that is in question; the word is the mirror of Being— and that the word is collapsing from within speaks of a more serious failure, one which affects the world and the hold we can have on the world. Things are also like an alphabet which once was clear but which is now eroding, like a language which yesterday had substance but today is torn across, of which only shreds are left. The word of poetry is made in the image of this earth, of this history which we live: sparse, ruined with emptiness, incomplete. If in so many poems by Octavio Paz we confront landscapes of flint and ash, shouldn't we hesitate to identify these landscapes with memories of a life and its travels? These high plateaus of broken stone, these deserts from the Orient or Mexico, represent in their cruel evidence something like the crystallization, at once metaphorical and tangible, of another abandonment that grips us at the edge of a world in so many ways *deserted*—a dead world, as we would say of a dead language, and one which offers our mental vision only "the signs of an alphabet in ruins." This is the birthplace of a poetry which knew itself from the beginning to be the approach, perhaps the sad apprehension of absence.

But that is also the end, for Octavio Paz, of what I will call the fascination with Mallarmé, if not of the discomfort which this fascination provokes. For the apprehension—even lucid—of a "default" in the world's being, the discovery of a metaphysical solitude lends itself to a nostalgia anchored in the deep memory, which we must relinquish each morning.

84

The old dream of an earlier Arcadia, of a fairy-tale country where meaning was one with the sign. . . . It is the dawn which wrests this watchman from the charm of a subjective night; which suggests other designs, less somber than those in which the self was enclosed, fascinated with its own labyrinths and shadows. Octavio Paz has always refused a narcissistic investigation of the subject—whether the shadowy call of a pure spirit or, more subtly, this profuse voice from the depths which, in the surrealist poem, speaks endlessly of itself.

We know the significance which his meeting with that "important passerby" of our century, André Breton, held for Octavio Paz. Paz himself has confirmed all that his own questioning, his poetic and even his political choices, owed during those years to the healthy mutiny of the word rising against the artifices and conventions of the concept. I do not mean to minimize the importance of this rebellion; but I think it necessary to define the ways in which Paz's attitude differs from a poetics with which he sympathized, but which he did not embrace. Where surrealism finds a second certainty—the discursive capacity of the unconscious—and builds on this certainty a system of perception and representation of the psychic universe, Octavio Paz sees an ambiguous return to rationality, a new law of the relations between consciousness and appearance, in short a reassuring logic which he cannot fully accept. To define the *surreal* and to set its limits, to find a touchstone within oneself—wasn't this, for Western thought, yet another return to the old mandate of the *logos,* wasn't this to push farther from us what fails and fades before speech? Surrealism did not question the authenticity of the deep self, still less its seemingly innocent epiphany in the word. Descending step by step, venturing in the dark of himself, Octavio Paz did not find this kind, ceaseless murmur, but only more darkness, more silence and more danger than in the space of the visible. "There is nothing in me but a great wound." A wound through which the sap escapes, the substance of the world and of the self—and which it would be futile to disguise, resorting to some turning in on oneself. The *space within* has not yielded all its monsters. . . . And not everyone can force them up from the depths and, like Henri Michaux, seize and conjure them.

If the poetry of our time, as Paz has said, cannot on its

own escape its isolation, poets owe it to themselves to fight, with all their strength, against a condition of moral isolation which compromises their desire for communication, which diminishes them, and which walls them into their own monologue. Throughout his great meditation on the poetic act, *El arco y la lira,* Octavio Paz reaffirms that "To be oneself, is to condemn oneself to mutilation, for humankind is the perpetual desire to be other." And still more explicitly in these phrases which question a certain egomania of contemporary poetry: "I aspire to Being, to the Being which changes, not to the salvation of the self." How far from this or that concern for individual salvation, the salvation which orients so many experiments today—intellectual, poetic, pictorial—experiments guided by an extravagant love of self. . . . And what a horizon stretches before the poem, what progress is promised to one who is no longer afraid to lose himself! I spoke earlier of the first impulse in Octavio Paz's writing, consubstantial with the poem's ascent, and which continues to set its direction. I will not distort the meaning of this impulse if I say that it represents a purgation—in the ascetic sense—of the passions, the subjective drives; the writer placing himself outside himself for the sake of what will be written through him. Octavio Paz has said again and again that poets are the ones who work "outside themselves." It is not that he exalts a delirium, or yields to the famous "derangement" *(dérèglement)* more or less concerted of all the senses which certain fragile disciples of Rimbaud have practiced, not to deliver themselves from this unhappy self, but to amplify it beyond measure and to better possess it. To wish himself "outside himself" is for Octavio Paz to refuse the limits which consciousness imposes, and more, to abandon all the refuges which our subjectivity, jealous of its quiet, does not cease to propose. It is finally and above all to respond to this vocation of *otherness* inherent in humankind, the prestige of its power which our fear disguises.

It would be necessary to concentrate, more than I can do here, on the first lines of certain poems where Paz's phrase seeks to be a departure from the being-there of the occasion, as also from the givens of the spirit, for "a walk through the underbrush," a sudden escape, a hesitant progress "among the corridors of time," with no light or guide—to take up the words of San Juan de la Cruz—except this call from the horizon, this other—improbable, inaccessible. And I think again of *El mono grámatico,* certainly a story of initiation, where the speaker, at the end of his pilgrimage of desire, may only reach the point of departure. Yet he is not disappointed, since the traveler's possessive consciousness has evaporated during this quest, and questioning of the word. Wasn't that already the wish of the author of *Piedra de sol,* when he wrote this hymn of new beginnings and cosmic returns?

> I return where I began
> I walk through the byways of myself
> Under an ageless sun

Poetry can never claim to have found an irrevocable definition of meaning. It may still have that ambition, but it must first cross the field of what cannot be located, must marry the evasive, must subject itself to the risks of an ocean in order to regain the land which was always promised and which has no name. Poetry—Octavio Paz tells us—is a movement *towards,* never a preestablished itinerary which could award itself the reassuring perspective of an *as far as.* And if the unappeased *I* of the poet aspires to become that *other* which Rimbaud dreamt, he cannot attain his dream except by that abandon of self and by the loss even of the memory of loss. Poetry is a bow aimed towards the improbable, but if it is not now for us to reach the target, still the arrow is new in our hands.

☆

It is the presence of death which we find at the threshold of this journey undertaken by the thought and poetry of Octavio Paz. Moving and unmoving, solemn and furtive, death enters—as, always alive, it enters the flesh—the heart of the words which refuse it. Octavio Paz does not believe in the god who came with the ships from Europe, who claims to redeem, and complete what's left undone, save Being from its wound or from its blasphemy. But Paz reveres a dark force which rules us and which we must not oppose, but accept with open eyes. "The dead do not exist, only Death, our

mother." We can feel sure that it is not a taste for the archae-
ological restoration of a culture, its religious imagery and its
rituals which has led Paz to give the Aztecs' cosmology and
their anthropological vision a privileged place in his thought
and, from early in his career, in his poems. Christianity could
not vanquish the old mysteries in Mexico any more than it
could in Asia; unable to convert them, it could only give a
name to the great terror of things. Octavio Paz has rejected
the too simple assurances of Christianity in order to hear the
lessons of the sacred Serpent. Quetzalcóatl does not fear
death or despise it; death is not a place of despair or the physical sign of a punishment. He passes through death—in order
to join the two aspects of being and to fuse them. He gives
himself to secret liturgies of the sun; he offers life, in the
guise of death. Octavio Paz has long contemplated this demi-
urge of astral and terrestrial revolutions: *Piedra de sol,* among
other poems, bears the sign of the crowned and rampant god.
Paz has done more than adhere to this highest figure among
Mexican deities, figure which has in fact nourished his experience and his writing. I will leave it to the commentators to
verify certain correspondences which seem obvious to me and
which, moreover, Paz has discussed. I believe his return to the
great drama of pre-Columbian consciousness has confirmed
and comforted a feeling in him, an intimate experience of
death, experience which has escaped the imperatives of a
Christian ethic—as it has abandoned the form and the spirit
of those Hispanic models which influenced the poet for a time.

For Spain, too, revered death. From Jorge Manrique to
Cernuda, Spain recognized in death something like a daily
companion, at once fearful and familiar, which ruins the
house of the real, but kindles a purer flame in the ruins. Octavio Paz loved these poets, who are almost unknown to the
French reader. Isn't it that they escape our language, and
even more the norms of understanding which our language
has prescribed for itself? Quevedo first of all, darkest soul
borne by Spain of the Golden Age, with whom Paz entered,
under the double sign of obsession and refusal, into a strange
dialogue. Admirable "suite" on the theme of love and death,
Homenaje y profanaciones seems in fact a sort of modern
counterpart to Quevedo's famous sonnet: *Cerrar podrá mis*

ojos. * . . . Homage rendered to a poet who ventured to the edge of the void, but also a will to separation, a desire to break the enchantment which, in Quevedo's poetry, subjects all the pomp of the sensible world to the power of usury, waste and the night. Paz has been faithful to the combat which Quevedo sustained against the shadowy wave, against the nothing which rises to assail man and the world. But this endless disillusionment, the complacence of this *desengaño* in its "kingdom of terror," could only incite Paz, disciple of the dawn, to uncover death's other face, of which Baroque Spain knew nothing: death, mistress of becoming, priestess of metamorphosis.

"Between birth and death, poetry introduces a possibility which is not the eternal life of religion or the eternal death of philosophy, but a living which implies and contains a dying." Rereading these phrases which Octavio Paz set at the end of his reflection, in *El arco y la lira,* on the poetic act, I will say that for Paz, too, the existential consciousness of death incites and directs a new burst of life. Only for those who rely on the principle of the excluded middle to guarantee the coherence of their logic is death unable to engender life. And isn't this, in fact, the law to which all Western thought has submitted, from the ontological declaration of Parmenides to the implacable injunctions of Hegel? One day we will have to admit that the conceptual dialectics we adhere to is a game of illusions, conciliating opposites which remain foreign to each other. The mystics have always known it—and a few poets as well, whose unreason, among our rational centuries, is still our salvation. San Juan de la Cruz, Sor Juana, Novalis, Nerval—it is from their dark progress, crossed with light, assailed by doubts, that Paz drew this knowledge, more of the soul than of the intellect—which sees in death the first source of Being in movement. "Death is the mother of forms," Octavio Paz wrote again in *Pasado en claro,* admirable book of an entirely metaphysical meditation. To accept this illumination, and not to reduce it to some paradox of the intellect, we must fight against ourselves. . . . And yet it is this illumination which will govern a poetics and a

---

*"My eyes will be able to close" from the poem "Amor constante más allá de la muerte" ("Unending Love Beyond Death") —Ed.

poetry always more insistent in the face of the old Greco-Roman systems of knowledge.

Octavio Paz shatters the stone matrix. His poetry carries an explosive charge which is turned, not on the poem itself but on the inertia of a world thought to be objective, and the notional structures which are forced to account for it. And that may be the only irremediable death—the impulse confined, a fixed quality of the moment, an identity taking pleasure in its own resemblance. The other, what is called physical death, is only the ordeal of a passage, the true place where the seed of things must decay, in order to give birth to what is already and what will be. The poetry of Octavio Paz does not forsake the sensible world; nor does Paz take refuge in an imaginary or unreal world, evasions which so often represent the last subterfuge of a poetics chafing at its limits. It is the "creatures" nearest us, in the universe which surrounds us—a tree, an instant of rain, this insect crying in the underbrush—that claim Paz's attention and a keenness of perception more speculative than visual. For Paz, to see and to retain these few images is already to raise them beyond a purely spatial and temporal vision, to discern their tangible presence and at the same time to feel that they may change. "Things are the same, and other."

We can certainly hear an echo of Buddhist doctrine and something of the great teaching of the Tao. But what is in Oriental thought an ascent beyond the body, silence and plenitude beyond gestures and words, regains an active dimension in Paz's writing, which seems to generate energy—a dimension which the Orient has nearly always refused. Not that I wish to minimize their enterprise or claim that it is easy to attain the transcendence of contradictions which alone permits one, according to the Upanishads, to experience the beatific state of *ananda,* delight of the spirit in the breast of the One. But I think it as much of an adventure, for a consciousness which operates in the ambiguous space of language—and our Latin idioms more than others, with their play of mental mirrors . . .—yes, I judge that the adventure is at least as perilous for a Western poet to escape the dualist idea of the world and to reunite in words what remains separated in things. For me, this is Paz's essential ambition, and the surprisingly modern grandeur of his poetry. The critique of

90

writing to which he has devoted himself does not lead, as so often in our poetry, to an ethics of suspicion, to the decor of signs which seek only to be persuaded of their futility and to deconstruct. Octavio Paz orients his search towards a less desolate horizon. If he distrusts the certainties of language, it is in order to reassert another power of which language has let itself be stripped—not to represent but to express the live flesh of things, to be of one substance with things, to rediscover itself, as in the first sun-filled morning, both word and presence. "Names seek a body." Words will no longer stay behind the glittering bars of abstractions. A world waits for them—only a mortal world, our world, but where a heart will beat again, where "We feel our lost unity beyond the invisible walls, the rotten masks which separate us from each other." Names seek a body—and the body, in its turn, seeks a name which will free it from the old fears of the self, from its silence.

☆

It is love which allows us this glimpse of our lost unity— and which may restore it to us, if we consent. Not the love which sanctifies itself in its difference, but that which is incarnate in the embrace of two bodies. The poetry of Octavio Paz seeks to become a passionate celebration, a fervor and even at times a furor of Eros. Since the eclipse of the natural myths, we have too often confused erotic poetry with a licentious confession, with a verbal exaltation whose only motivation seemed the private satisfaction of a sensuality. Octavio Paz has returned to eroticism some of its panicked seriousness, the signs of its truth. For him, love is more than the desire which carries individuals outside themselves—and withdraws them briefly from their solitude; it is a rebirth of the other, and through the intermediary of these bodies joining, the hope of a fusion with the protean substance of the world. Paz's most beautiful erotic poems, "Maithuna," *Blanco,* are also those in which the cosmic reality is revealed in all its transparence. As if by embracing a bare body, marrying its landscape, quenching its thirst, the reality of the world would become more tangible, its firmament fill with light above us, the conjunction of male and female stars endure in a single flash of light. The distance which subsisted between the self

and the other, between things and words, will now be effaced
in the act of love—mingling and fusion of You and Me in We
who are created indivisible. . . .

> The world is visible now in your body,
> Transparent in your transparence

In the new mythology generated by the poet, Eros is no
longer the futile god of the legends, blind and blinding. He
is once more the dazzled walker, the pilgrim hungering for
the absolute—and in his steps, as once for Orpheus, the dark
fails and the dead stones come alive. The world has found
its center again—not determined by a despotic consciousness
but by a will rising in each of us and which transcends us,
"an unnamed pronoun" which is Eros' force becoming a poem.

For poetry is nothing but the verbal transcription of a
loving order. This is, at any rate, the task which poetry must
accept once it chooses to escape a system of discursive relations, a parsimonious economy of concepts, symbols which
will never know suffering or terror. It has been said—a little
naively—that the words of the poem make love together. I
can accept that. . . . But words have every chance to make
love, in the image of bodies—each in accord with the other,
fusing into a single sentence, or simulating an encounter which
safeguards their autonomy while stimulating their pleasure.
Any authentic experience of poetry is, by its very nature,
erotic, because such an experience springs from a lack and is
illumined by its own desire. We can still distinguish, on the
one hand a narcissistic grammar of the poem, in love with its
own legibility, turned in on itself—the writing of Valéry or of
Saint-John Perse, to cite only a few examples from our century—and on the other hand, a verbal adventure, generous in
its flight, open to a larger perception which seems to carry
the poem past its intention, to mystify it. I think of Reverdy,
of Jouve, of Breton at times. . . . We rediscover in Paz this
breath of the poetic phrase, and this span: a trembling of the
word, a subterranean impulse of the syntax which subverts
the categories of discourse in favor of a freer, more generous
progress—all the more likely to contain in its flight something
of the world's ungoverned movement.

Love is an abundance of desiring language; a profusion,

an extravagant expense of the self, a wealth always renewed. For Octavio Paz, the image is the unquestionable manifestation, at the climax of writing, of that eroticism which sets the entire universe in motion, which carries it off—live matter, heart and spirit—in a whirlwind of metamorphosis. What intrigues Paz's reader from the start, what will always fascinate us, is an explosion, a fertile exchange among forms and figures which seem to give birth to one another, to separate, rejoin, burst into a thousand suns of signs, into constellations of metaphors, into a stardust of metonymies. . . . But the image, as it is practiced here does not depend on an arbitrary proceeding of the intellect, any more than it leads to the caprices of an imaginary world. I have already mentioned the attachment which Paz feels for the tenor, one could almost say the savor of natural phenomena, and to what degree the fantastic and the arbitrary are foreign to a poetry rooted in the real. The same is true for the elaboration of the image, and here again we may stress what distinguishes Paz's method from certain surrealist directives, perhaps what most clearly divides him from surrealism. For André Breton, the image was the way to provoke an explosion which would be healthy for the spirit. The shock of two "aberrant entities" would, Breton thought, demolish the lovely house of our reason. . . . The exquisite corpse, the famous conjunction of an umbrella and a sewing machine on a dissection table, have taken on an emblematic value. Could Breton, conceiving the image in a way which is, after all, analytic, achieve his ends? It is not certain that the almost mechanical arrangement of the imaginary—that "systematic illumination of the high places of the unconscious," according to Breton's definition, escapes so readily from rationality, or that it acquires those hermeneutic virtues which some have thought the surrealist image held. Surrealism too quickly identified the unusual with the mysterious. The contact which Paz maintained with surrealism has not prevented him from taking an opposite tack. Certainly the image remains for him the union of realities or ideas which the principle of non-contradiction opposes; but his image does not aim to exacerbate their differences; instead it gathers together the profusion of situations, emotions and circumstances in the hospitality of the One. I would even say the image has a *religious* vocation for Paz, in the first sense of the term. It does not disperse, but gathers in, it seeks to bring together our different approaches, to fuse our sights.

Through images, the poetry of Octavio Paz approaches a *reconciliation*—the hope of all unitive philosophies—and not a problematic conciliation of opposites. He escapes in this way, and even at the level of language, the intolerance which has been the pride of Western thought, in which each conscious subject is confined within its domain, and perceives others only in the belligerent relations of supremacy or submission. By affirming that "things are the same and other," Octavio Paz not only blurs the categories we hold to—that was surrealism's objective—he captures the naturant energy of the universe in "cages of light where identity is annulled among likenesses, difference in contradictions." For Octavio Paz, the poem is an insurrection of the word against the conventions and the precarious equilibriums of the concept. More, it is the insurrection of sense against the repressive system of particular meanings. Faced with a rhetoric of reification, with ideologies of the beautiful totality, the poem rediscovers itself as *uprising,* at once rebellion and rebirth. Uprising of the sensible world, towards a transparence which is more than an intelligibility promised to the mind. Uprising of Being towards a *truth,* the truth of which Rimbaud spoke, present at last *in one body and soul.*

Poetry must now free itself, as much as possible, from its fascination with the figure of destruction in whom Mallarmé recognized a guardian angel, his Beatrice. . . . If poets have come to distrust, and not without reason, the capacity of language to recover a real and not a simulated presence, they must also fear that the conscience and conduct of negativity, taken to extremes, may be lost in mutism, or, more perniciously, may end in verbal terrorism, in a didactics of overabundance or of emptiness. Octavio Paz affirms that if poetry is first of all the cruel ordeal of separation, it must transcend this negative stage of the "Deus absconditus" and force itself, once more, to gather the sparse words of the real in a single phrase—always threatened, always to be born—of certainty. The poet refuses the dispersion of sensible phenomena which others have made a fatality. As Eros reunites the You and the Me in a single pronoun—a single presence—so the poem is a moment of fervor, an act of faith which will carry the poet "to the other side of night where I am you, where we are others." For words are that much more our own if, in the exchange with others, in their recognition, they can once more belong to everyone. The language of poetry cannot be reduced to an idiolect, to a system of signs which is indecipherable for those who do not hold the key. Poetry is, in the real sense of the term, the creation of a "common place," the affirmation of a shared word, the reassertion of an unbroken history.

Paz's interest in the Holy Books of Buddhism has not encouraged him into a salutary detachment from his body, beyond the shared constraints of time. If he declares history to be a "punishment" inflicted on humankind, he immediately adds, "it is also the place of the ordeal"—a place we must not abandon. Nowhere more clearly than in the poems of *Ladera este,* among these landscapes buried in the dust of centuries, do we hear the concerns and the unanswered questions of our time. For even by the sacred rivers, in the meditation of the immutable, there is no certainty which can silence the immense clamor of the poor. Nor is there a word, not even the most attentive, which can cure their sorrow. But let the poem be this welcome, let it be open to the despair of the world; let each one's pain become everyone's scandal. And perhaps, at the end of the road, once the frontiers of illusions, of false knowledge have been crossed, we will be able to greet a birth, to say with Paz, who will never accept the disabusement of each night, or the lies, that the earth is intact, and love must be reinvented.

> The day
> Is a vast clear word.
> And the world is real.
> I see,
> I inhabit a transparence.

trans. from the French by Susanna Lang

☆   ☆   ☆

John Cage

WHITE ON *BLANCO* FOR O. P.

el cOmienzo
Con
los ojos abierTos   inocente
promiscuA
alto en su Vara
cabeza en una pIca
un girasOl

un Pulso
oleAje de sílabas húmedas
aguZar

silenciOs
hasta la transparenCia
de Tu
pAís
de espejos en Vela
las altas fIeras
rueda el ríO seminal

Por
lA percepción
de reses de ceniZa

mugen lOs árboles
enCadenados
Te golpeo cielo
tierrA
Verdea
se esparce árIda
Ondulación se levanta

se Persigue
girAndo
aZules

gira el anillO beodo
    giran los Cinco
        senTidos
            Alrededor de la amatista
            Veo
        la músIca
    el númerO cristalizado

        no Pienso
    que pienso lA cara en blanco
en tus semejanZas

            yO soy tu lejanía
            Caes
        de Tu nombre
        A tu cuerpo
        Vulva la palabra
    la hendIdura encarnada en
        dOs sílabas enamoradas

        tu cuerPo son los cuerpos
        del instAnte
    olor desnudeZ

    en las manOs de aire
            Comida por mi
        fesTín
    de nieblA
            reVoloteando
        entre las líneas de la página
el pensamientO

        que nos Protege los protege
        sus rAmas acallan
            jaZmín y ala

de cuervO
y las apariCiones
un Tejido
de lenguAje
antes de eVaporarse
la realIdad y
sus resurrecciOnes

el esPíritu
es unA
el comienZo el cimiento

Yves Bonnefoy

IN THE LURE OF THE THRESHOLD

Strike,
Strike forever.

In the lure of the threshold.

At the sealed door,
At the empty phrase.
In the iron, waking
Only these words—the iron.

In language, in that darkness.

In the one who keeps
Unmoving vigil, there
At his table, charged
With signs, with glimmers. And who is called

Three times, but does not rise.

. . . .

In the gathering, where there was no
Cause for celebration.

In the misshapen grain
And the parched wine.

In the hand which holds
An absent hand.

In the uselessness
Of memory.

In the writing, hastily
Gathered in the night

And in the words which have burnt out
Even before the dawn.

. . . .

In the mouth which wants
From another mouth
The honey which no summer
Can ripen.

In the brusque note which
Sharpens
Till it is almost—glacial
—The passage.

Then the insistence of
The silenced note,
Its bare wave broken
Beneath the star.

In a star reflected
On iron.
In the anguish of bodies
Not finding each other.

Strike, late.

These lips desiring
Even when the blood flows

The hand striking with full force
Even when
The arm is only scattered
Ashes.

. . . .
. . . .

Deeper in the black earth
Than the dog,
The ferryman throws himself, crying aloud
Towards the other shore.
Full of mud your mouth,
Your eyes devoured,
Push your boat for us
Through the matter of this world.
You do not know what depth your pole finds,
Nor what current:
Nor what will light the words
Seized with black, the words in the book.

Deeper than the dog
Which is poorly covered
They bury you, boatman,
In the cloak of signs.
They speak to you, and give you
One or two keys, the useless
Map of another land.
You listen, your eyes already turned
Towards the dark water.
You listen to the earth
Which falls from their shovels.

Deeper than the dog
which died yesterday,
Boatman, they will plant
Your phosphorescence.
The hands of young girls
Have loosened the earth
Under the stalk which bears
The gold of future seedings.
You could still see their arms,

Heavily shadowed,
And the swelling of their breasts
Under the tunics.
Laughter kindles up above
But you are leaving.

You were thrown bleeding
Into the light;
You opened your eyes, crying
To name the day;
But the day is not spoken
When already the curtain of blood
Is falling, with a dull noise
Over the light.
Laughter kindles up above,
Red in the thickness
Which breaks apart.
Turn your eyes from the fires
Of our shore.

Deeper than the fire
Which does not catch
Is set the fire's witness, the undeciphered,
On a bed of leaves.
Faces turned toward us,
Readers of signs,
What unheard wind from the other side
Will force a sound from them?
What hesitant hands,
As if on new ground,
Will take, and leaf through
The shadow of pages?
What thoughtful hands,
As if having found?

. . . .

Oh lean down, comfort us,
Cloud
Of a smile
Which stirs in this clear face.

For the one who was cold
Against the shore,
Be Pharaoh's daughter
With her servants,

Whose red cloths
The water, when it is still
Not dawn,
Reflects in reverse.

. . . .

And as a hand
Sorts on a table
The grain which has nearly germinated
From the dark chaff,

And as in the water of dark wood
The hand, in taking, is doubled
By a reflection, where the meaning
Suddenly is present,

Gather, that they may sleep
In your Word,
Our words which the wind tears
With its storms.

. . . .

"Have you come to drink of this wine,
I will not let you drink.
Have you come to learn of this dark
Bread, burnt with the fire of a promise,
I will not let a light shine there.
Have you come, if only
That the water appease you, a little warm water
Drunk in the night, where other lips have drunk before
Between the unmade bed and the simple earth,
I will not let you touch the glass.
Have you come, that the child may shine
Above the flame which seals him
In the immortality of the April hour
Where he can laugh; and you, where the bird lights
In the welcoming hour which has no name;
I will not let you raise your hands above the hearth where
                                      my clear fire reigns.

"Have you come,
I will not let you enter.
Do you ask,
I will not let you know the name that is formed by your lips."

. . . .

Deeper than the stones
Which the workman standing
On the wall tears out,
Late in the night.

Deeper than the crow's flank, the crow
Which marks the fog with its rust
And passes crying in a dream,
Blackest of black earth.

Deeper than the summer
Broken by the shovel.
Deeper than the cry
In another dream,

He throws himself, crying out, the one
Who represents us,
The hope which throws a shadow
On the origin,

And the one unity, this movement
Of his body—when all at once,
With his weight thrown against the pole,
He forgets us.

. . . .

We, the voice beaten back
By the wind of words.
We, the work which is torn
By their whirlwind.

For if I approach you, who have spoken
—Debris, rustlings,
Echos, the room is empty.
Is it "another's," the call which answers me,
Or still myself?
And under the many-echoed vault
Am I no more
Than one of echo's shafts, loosed
Against these things?

We
Among sounds,
We
One of them.

Loosening themselves
From the crumbling wall;
Making of themselves a hollow,
An opening, empty of self;
Flushing,
Swelling with a distant plenitude.

. . . .

Look at this torrent,
Thrown crying into the deserted summer
—And yet, unmoving,
It is the team of horses, rearing
And the blind face.
Listen.
The echo does not surround the noise but is in the noise
Is its canyon.
Its cliffs,
The funnel-shaped opening where its waters break,
The saxifrage
Pass from your eyes with an eagle's
Cry—final.
You cannot know
Where the breast of the beast is striking, the breast of
                                    the water's voice;
But let yourself be carried, light-dazzled,
By its raucous wing.

We
At the burst of sound,
We
Carried.

We—yes—when the torrent
Throws, rolls and seizes again
With its broken hands
The absolute,—the stones.

The predator
Crying out
At the crest of its flight,
Turns on itself, rends its own breast.
And from the breast divided by the dark beak
Flows the void.
At the crest of the Word there is still noise,
And in our works
The surge of another noise.
But at the crest of the noise, the light changes.

. . . .

All things seen,—these weak forms,
—Are erased, unwritten,
Embers, where the call
Of other lands will pass.

And the lightning is at peace
Above the trees,
As is the breast where death and sleep
Move in a dream,

And the night of the world
Is burning—a color,
Like a painted cloth
Spreading in black water

When the image
Suddenly parts the current,
Crying its seed, the fire
Against a pole.

. . . .

Hour
subtracted now from the sum.
Presence
Undeceived of death. Bulb
Which kneels in silence
And burns
With a refracted light, shaken
By the summitless night.

I listen to you
Hum in the nothing of the work
Which toils through the world.
I hear the trampling
of calls
Which pasture in the flaming bulb.

I take the earth by handfuls
In this flared opening, with its smooth walls,
Where there is no bottom
Before dawn.
I listen to you, I take
All the earth
In your rope basket. Outside,
It is still the time of sorrow
Before the image.
In the closed hand which is outside
The seed of the things of this world
Has begun to germinate.

. . . .
. . . .

The Boatman
Who touches your shoulder
With his thoughtful pole
And you, already the one whom the night covers
While your pole searches in vain
For the river's bottom

Which will be found, or lost,
Who can hope, who can promise?
Lean down, see all of a face
Appear in the water

Like a fire catching, at the reflection
Of your shoulder.

> *From* Dans le leurre du seuil
> *trans. from the French by Susanna Lang*

Carlos Fuentes

HOMENAJE TO OCTAVIO PAZ

Octavio Paz is certainly the greatest living poet of the Spanish language. From *Luna silvestre* (1933) to *Vuelta* (1976) the corpus of Paz's poetic creation has grown simultaneously in several directions. First, as an inner renewal of the Spanish language, then as an outward connection of our renewed language with that of the world. By making our language a vehicle of human communication (by which I mean a communication of all that is left unsaid by the loudspeakers of yesterday and today: dogma, publicity, authority speaking in the name of history, the brutal or subtle forms of repression), Paz permits Spanish Americans to speak for all humanity and with all peoples. His poetics is thus an art of civilization, a motion of encounters. Within himself, Paz the poet encounters Paz the philosopher. This is not a gratuitous meeting. It is essential to his *démarche:* poetry as a form of thought, thought as a form of poetry. Literature in Paz becomes a synonym of civilization: both are a network of communicating vessels, and only the totality of communication can reveal the true face of humankind. There are no privileged centers of culture, race or ideology; the essential orphanhood of our times is faced by the poetry and the philosophy of Octavio Paz as a challenge to be surmounted by a renewal of the flow of human knowledge, interrupted by sundry deterministic or reductivist concepts of time, progress and happiness. I know of no other living writer who has so powerfully expressed the existence of a plurality of times, a plurality of possibilities for harmony and truth, outside the limited range of our inherited dogmas. In his work there is a miraculous meeting of all invented times (original, circular, linear, instantaneous) in a simultaneous space: the written page. The conscience of this multiplicity of human times in Paz is a conscience of the uniqueness of human destiny, composed of a plurality of living cultures. In Paz, the ancient civilizations of the Americas meet and fuse with the ancient civilizations of the Orient and the civilization of the West merges with the civilizations of Asia, Africa and the Americas in order to enrich and be enriched beyond the stagnant *hubris* of its old metropolitan pretensions. Yucatán, Angkor and Paestum become a new space, a reunion where we can simultaneously hear the voices of the *Popol Vuh,* Matsuo Basho and Baudelaire, see the forms of Bonampak, Hokusai and Marcel Duchamp, participate in the dialogue between Heraclitus, Lao Tzu and Nietzsche. I know of no other contemporary writer who has given so much of his individual expression to a poetical form that transcends him in order to establish the common voice of the hidden fraternity of civilizations. Octavio Paz is a great poet because he is able to give resonance to the many through the one.

☆   ☆   ☆

Allen W. Phillips

A TRIBUTE TO OCTAVIO PAZ
(Notes on *Children of the Mire*)

It would be highly presumptuous to specify in these brief
pages what so many writers and critics owe to Octavio Paz,
universally read poet and essayist, whose voluminous and varied publications now span a period of some forty odd years
of intense creative activity and fertile change. Leaving aside
for the moment his impressive verse, characterized by its
sweep, verbal brilliance and originality of vision, I am primarily concerned here with an ancillary activity of Paz, none the
less creative however, and which constitutes already a considerable portion of his entire work: literary thought and
criticism.

Paz's critical commentaries (as his translations as well)
are essentially creative and frequently offer close readings
which significantly illuminate the meaning and artistic execu-
tion of difficult texts. Direct analysis of the poem is characteristic: a sonnet of Mallarmé, a long and complex modern
poem of Apollinaire or an unfinished baffling lyric of López
Velarde are noteworthy examples. Paz is neither a literary
historian nor a systematic scholar but a highly sensitive
reader, committed and intellectually honest, who gives his
readers, aided by a vast knowledge and unfailing intuition, a
true insight into art. He clarifies and judges simultaneously,
without shrinking from the delicate task of appraisal; he is
impartial, yes, but never rejects his own emotional response
to the work of art.[1] A most striking feature of his recent critical work is its vast cultural structure, embracing all literature

---

[1] One of the best definitions that Paz gives us as to the mission and re-
sponsibilities of the critic is to be found in the essay "Tamayo: de la
crítica a la ofrenda," *Puertas al campo* (México, 1966), pp. 215–226.
In this connection, another text should be mentioned: "Sobre la crítica," *Corriente alterna* (México, 1967), pp. 39–44. For a general con-
sideration of the literary criticism of Paz, see my treatment in the early
pages of "Octavio Paz: crítico de la poesía mexicana moderna," *Cinco
estudios sobre literatura mexicana moderna* (México, 1974), pp. 145–181.

and art, modern and ancient, exotic or indigenous, not to mention other disciplines such as linguistics or anthropology. These credentials lie behind and give added range to his creative and intuitive powers. Some readers might be suspicious of the perilous but always thought provoking analogies which Paz at times establishes as he cuts boldly across time and space, ages and national boundaries.

For professional reasons it is perhaps only natural for me to confess that I am particularly interested in what Paz has to say about the poets who, in various epochs and different languages, have broken with their tradition to seek new creative roads and employ an equally renovative language for literary expression. His comments on a family of writers such as Laforgue, Lugones, López Velarde, for example, and on more modern poets having the stature of Eliot and Pound would be an excellent case in point—further proof of Paz's thesis of interdependency in the literary world. His pages on modernism and specifically Mexican literature from Sor Juana to the present have been particularly influential in my own thinking. My constant return to Laforgue, to his irony and detached vision of the world expressed in a dual language of poetic and prosaic tint, is in no small part fostered by Paz himself. To reaffirm the brilliance of his synthetic summing up of the ideals of certain literary movements (romanticism, modernism, surrealism), or generations (the Mexican *Contemporáneos* or even his own more recent *Taller)* and to single out sharply honed fragments devoted to individual artists who interest him is to say again the most obvious. The extensive essays on Darío, López Velarde and other figures of the Hispanic tradition, the briefer but no less penetrating pages on Reyes, Tablada, Guillén and many others are models of literary appreciation at their very best. Nor should we fail to mention at least in passing Octavio Paz's sustained interest in the plastic arts.

The incisive and dazzling aphorisms which are want to sum up his thought, generally complex and often paradoxical, constitute another typical trait of his critical technique. These succinct phrases often appear at the end of long paragraphs, and what critic, for example, can equal for clarity, simplicity but at the same time depth of vision the often quoted words about Hispanic modernism: "Modernism began as an aesthetic of rhythm and ended as a rhythmic vision of the universe."[2] But once again the impact of his analogies, never artificially limited by nationalities nor by languages, are what strike me as being so startling, however dangerous the game may be. It is the one only suited to the highly prepared and original intellect. The truth of the matter is that both the real and authentic dialogue, literary and artistic, about which Paz so often talks is in fact clearly established in critical essays such as those he has given us in half a dozen closely knit books, often fragmentary in nature, with the exception perhaps of the more organic *The Bow and the Lyre* and the recent *Children of the Mire*.

The foregoing personal generalizations give a rough indication of the range and intrinsic value of Paz's critical writings. However, in the interests of brevity, let us add that despite the continual evolution of the poet's thought and search (he might prefer the word *exploration*) there is a certain immobility or rather a fixed quality in the basic aesthetic concerns which interest him. They can be reduced, I believe, to several closely linked problems which form the cornerstone of his paradoxically flexible artistic doctrine. We note at first glance in Paz a deep preoccupation for a universal and cosmopolitan literature, implying at the same time the absolute necessity for never ending communication among the creators of modern art. And even more specifically the fervent wish to isolate and describe the very being and exact nature of the contemporary poem, which in itself is constantly creating other poems and other meanings. Paz is passionately concerned, not only with literary dialogue and contact between writers, as well as their experimentation with new techniques, but at the same time he points toward an ideal for the study or reading (and even teaching) of literature as a series of collective styles and patterns which, on crossing national borders, meet to constitute through the ages forms of expression and

---

[2] I quote from the translation by Lysander Kemp and Margaret S. Peden of the essay on Darío included in *The Siren and the Seashell* (Austin, 1976), p. 30. The same phrase appears in *Children of the Mire* in a slightly different form: "Modernism began as a search for verbal rhythm and ended in a vision of the universe as rhythm." (P. 95.) All quotations and references are from *Children of the Mire. Modern Poetry from Romanticism to the Avant-Garde* (Harvard University Press: Cambridge, 1974), translated by Rachel Phillips.

artistic modes which repeat themselves in a cyclical manner. Paz appears to reject a linear and chronological idea of artistic history and prefers to accept a different approach.[3] The poem is unique but it is never isolated, and in his studies of literature Paz seizes upon and exploits contradictions or separations as neatly as he perceives the contrary, namely unities or similarities. Let us try to imagine for a moment the brilliance of a student of Hispanic literature with the intellectual capacity and artistic knowledge to approach a method of reading which cannot fail to be suggested in the following words of Octavio Paz, although any pedagogical intent is, of course, far from his intent in writing them:[4]

> To envisage the myths as phrases or parts of a discourse that would encompass all the myths of a civilization is a disconcerting but nevertheless a salutory idea. Applied to literature, for example, it would reveal a different and perhaps more exact image of what we consider to be tradition. Instead of being a succession of names, works and tendencies, tradition would be converted into a system of significant relations: a language. The poetry of Góngora would not only be something after Garcilaso and prior to Rubén Darío, but rather a text in dynamic relation with other texts. We would read Góngora not as an isolated text but in its context: those works which determine it and those that his poetry itself determines. If we conceived of poetry written in Spanish more as a system than as history, the meaning of the works which constitute it would not depend as much on chronology nor on our point of view as on the relationship existing between the texts themselves and the movement of the system. The significance

---

[3] This is a major theme in the critical writings of Octavio Paz and appears and reappears in his work. Within the present framework, see *Children of the Mire* (pp. 120–121) and the short essay "Literatura de fundación," *Puertas al campo,* pp. 11–19, which has been translated by Lysander Kemp.

[4] Octavio Paz, *Claude Lévi-Strauss o el neuvo festín de Esopo* (México, 1967 and 1969), pp. 131–132, note 3. I have made for the purpose of this note a rough version of the text in question since the official translation is not presently available to me.

of Quevedo does not come to an end in his own work nor in that of the *conceptistas* of the XVII century. Even the sense of his writing is to be found more fully in some poem of Vallejo although, of course, what the Peruvian poet says is not identical to what Quevedo meant. Sense is transformed without disappearing: each permutation, on changing it, prolongs it. The relation between one work and another is not merely chronological or rather that relation is variable and constantly alters chronology . . . The idea of Lévi-Strauss invites us to see Spanish literature not as a conglomerate of works but rather as a single work. This is a system, a language in movement and in relation with other systems: namely, other European literatures and their American heritage.

In the present pages, however, I cannot discuss but only mention in passing these fruitful and stimulating considerations which have had a deep impact on me and, I presume, on other literary scholars, particularly those dealing with the Hispanic tradition. Without losing them completely from view, I propose to limit myself here to a few random remarks on two subjects: irony and analogy, terms generally in conflict and opposition. They seem, nevertheless, to be at the very heart of *Children of the Mire,* the title accorded the Charles Eliot Norton Lectures given by Octavio Paz at Harvard University in 1971–1972. This book, admirably translated by Rachel Phillips, in many ways reads like a summing up and certainly as a restatement of many of the fundamental aesthetic concerns which the author has expressed on earlier occasions.

Both at the beginning and again at the end of *Children of the Mire* Paz devotes considerable space to a series of remarks about our modern age, which, being born of negation, is one of criticism and change that interrupts continuity at a dizzying pace. However, what most concerns us here is the basic duality of irony and analogy. Modern irony, an invention of the Romantics, is lucidly described by the essayist in the following manner:

. . . The religions and loves of the Romantics are heresies, syncretisms, apostasies, blasphemies, conversions. Romantic ambiguity has two modes, in the musical meaning of

the word: irony, which introduces the negation of subjectivity into the realm of objectivity; and anguish, which
drops a hint of nothingness into the fullness of being.
Irony reveals the duality of what seemed whole, the
split in what is identical, the other side of reason; it is
the disruption of the principle of identity. Anguish
shows that existence is empty, that life is death, that
heaven is a desert; it is the fracturing of religion (pp.
44–45).

> ... irony, humor, intellectual paradox; and also the
> poetic paradox, the image. Both appear in all the Ro-
> mantics. The predilection for the grotesque, the hor-
> rible, the strange, the sublime, and the bizarre; the aes-
> thetic of contrasts; the pact between laughter and tears,
> prose and poetry, agnosticism and faith; the sudden
> changes of mood, the antics—everything that turns each
> Romantic poet into an Icarus, a Satan, and a clown is
> essentially anguish and irony ... (p. 46)

Chapter four of *Children of the Mire* is entitled precisely
"Analogy and Irony" (pp. 58–77) and is therefore most vital
to the main concern in the present comments. The true religion of modern poetry, especially from Romanticism to Surrealism, is Paz claims the poetics of analogy, and in this connection he writes:

> ... The belief in correspondences between all beings and
> worlds predates Christianity, crosses the Middle Ages,
> and, through Neoplatonism, illuminism, and occultism,
> reaches the nineteenth century. Since then, secretly or
> openly, it has never failed to nourish Western poets,
> from Goethe to Balzac, from Baudelaire and Mallarmé
> to Yeats and Pessoa. (p. 55)

and, on being well aware of the permanence of analogy to
thought and to poetic expression, Paz will then say in synthesis:

> ... Poetry is one of the manifestions of analogy; rhymes
> and alliterations, metaphors and metonymies are modes
> of operation in analogical thought. A poem is a spiral
> sequence which turns ceaselessly without ever returning

completely to its beginning. If analogy turns the universe into a poem, a text made up of oppositions which become resolved in correspondences, it also makes the poem a universe. Thus, we can *read* the universe, we can *live* the poem. . . . Poetry is the *other* coherence, made not of reason but of rhythms. And there is a moment when the correspondence is broken; there is a dissonance which in the poem is called "irony" and in life "mortality." Modern poetry is awareness of this dissonance within analogy (p. 56).

Paz's discussion of Romanticism, which purported to unite the extremes of "art and life, timeless antiquity and contemporary history, imagination and irony" (p. 59), clearly emphasizes inspiration and passion ("a turning inward of the poetic vision," p. 61) in its ideology and way of life. The movement, of course, was much more than a change of style and outlook. This change in beliefs was inspired by analogy: "Analogy conceives of the world as rhythm: everything corresponds because everything fits together and rhymes. It is not only a cosmic syntax, it is also prosody. If the universe is a script, a text, or a web of signs, the rotation of these signs is governed by rhythm. Correspondence and analogy are but names for universal rhythm" (p. 63).[5]

The complex and conflictive aesthetic of Baudelaire, built upon attractions and rejections, is vital to the understanding of this question and is an almost obligatory point of reference here. Analogy is the very center of Baudelaire's concept of art, a moveable center as we shall see, but he was very much aware naturally of its counterpart: irony. Let us briefly try to follow Paz's reasoning. Baudelaire conceived of the world as a language, ever changing and varying, always different but yet the same, and it is logical then that the poem is a reading of reality (p. 72), which in its attempt to decipher the pluralities of this reality creates a new code or cipher. Analogy or the awareness of correspondences exists by virtue of differences:

. . . it [analogy] redeems them, it makes their existence

---

[5] In this context, the pages about Rubén Darío are very signficant: *The Siren and the Seashell*, pp. 28–30.

tolerable. Each poet and each reader is a solitary consciousness: analogy is the mirror in which they are reflected. And so, analogy does not imply the unity of the world, but its plurality, no man's sameness, but his perpetual splitting away from himself. Analogy says that everything is the metaphor of something else, but in the sphere of identity there are no metaphors. Differences are obliterated in unity, and otherness disappears (p. 73).

This is all very well and pluralities do become intelligible or resolved, but Paz hastens to warn us again that Baudelaire conceives of modern poetry as being nurtured by a special sense of strange beauty: the unique, the singular and the grotesque. And it is obvious that here we are faced not with the poetics of analogy but with those of irony, which are contradictory and irreconcilable. At the end of the chapter Paz alludes to Dante and then to Mallarmé, both of whom perceived the cosmos in the image of a book, but the critic is at the same time quick to add the following with reference to the modern poet, who knows that the world is neither a book nor intelligible: ". . . Negation, criticism, irony, these also constitute knowledge, though of the opposite kind to Dante's. A knowledge which is not the contemplation of otherness from the vantage point of unity, but the vision of breaking away from unity. An abysmal knowledge, an ironic knowledge" (p. 76). Thus the conflict seems to boil down to the disparate nature of universal analogy and an ironic concept of the world. Again we are back with Baudelaire, Laforgue et al. and even looking ahead to the remarkable Valle-Inclán, who was so conscious of this anomaly as can be readily seen in *La lámpara maravillosa* and other significant texts.

In this context, it would not exceed the limits of the present note to refer to modernismo which Paz now calls "our real Romanticism" (p. 88). He suggests, as he has done so often in the past, still another answer to those who cling to the outmoded notion that modernist aesthetics and style were merely superficial or decorative:

. . . Our critics and historians have been insensitive to the contradictory dialectic uniting positivism and modernismo. Consequently, they insist upon seeing the latter only as a literary trend and, above all, as a cosmopolitan and rather superficial style. No, modernismo answered spiritual needs. Or, more precisely, it was the answer of imagination and sensibility to the positivist drought. Only because it answered needs of the soul could it be a true poetic movement. . . . Among us modernismo was the response needed to contradict the spiritual vacuum created by the positivistic criticism of religion and metaphysics; nothing was more natural than that Spanish American poets should be attracted by the French poetry of this period. They discovered in it not only the novelty of a language but a sensibility and an aesthetic impregnated with the analogical vision of the Romantic and occultist traditions. . . . (pp. 88–89).

On this basis, then, it is not hard to bridge the gap as Paz had already done in his prior essay on Darío when he refers here to the new rhythmic elements introduced by the Nicaraguan poet and his followers, affirming without hesitation: ". . . this resurrection of meters coincided with the appearance of a new sensibility, which eventually proved to be a return to the *other* religion: analogy. Poetic rhythm is none other than a manifestation of the universal rhythm. Analogy is a rhythmic vision of the universe; before becoming an idea, it is a verbal experience. If the poet hears the universe as a language, he also *utters* the universe" (p. 94). Of course, these beliefs are immediately related as before in "The Siren and the Seashell" to the occultist tradition which is central to the modernist world outlook. In a clever phrase, Paz returns again to the antinomy: "The modernista tragicomedy is composed of a dialogue between the body and death, analogy and irony" (p. 96).[6] Despite the great importance conceded by Martí to

---

[6] Paz rejects, perhaps with good reason, the use of the term *postmodernismo* and in this connection he argues cogently: ". . . Postmodernismo was not what followed modernismo—which was actually vanguardismo—but a criticism of modernismo within the movement itself. It was an individual reaction on the part of various poets. Another movement did not start with them; modernismo ended with them. They were its critical consciousness, the consciousness of its ending. Moreover, the characteristic features of these poets—irony, colloquial language, already had appeared in the leading modernista poets. Finally, there is literally no space, in a chronological sense, for this pseudo-movement:

universal analogy[7], I was surprised to find quoted at the end of chapter five (p. 101) a poem of the Cuban writer in which Paz stresses its modernity and at the same time accords special emphasis to an original line which could not have been written, according to the critic, prior to the time of Martí. The phrase in question: "The universe / speaks better than man."[8]

The final chapter of *Children of the Mire* is aptly entitled "The Closing of the Circle" (pp. 102–164) and here Paz deals with the later trends of the avant-garde, relating them first of all to Romanticism as he points out the intensification and extreme nature of change characterizing most recent times. The primary struggle for the writer: the opposition of art and life (p. 112). The revolt is both individual and social; the vogue for experimentation is often transmuted into order (p. 146); and, after about 1945, Paz sees in the *vanguardia* a kind of disillusionment (pp. 146–147). Having insisted again on the duality of analogy and irony as symptomatic of modern poetry (p. 136), Octavio Paz brings his lectures to an appropriate close as he returns to the modern age of crisis and schism, change and permutation. Negation, he feels now, is no longer as creative as it once may have been (p. 149). Poetry and art are not coming to an end. The modern era is. The idea of *otherness* is stressed as the voice of the poet disappears behind the voice of language (p. 160) and the experiment of *Renga* is recalled. A final note pops up as the book enters into its last pages, a note which tends to confirm our contention that the interplay between analogy and irony is

---

if modernismo died out around 1918 and the vanguardia began at about that time, where can we put the *postmodernistas*? And yet the change was remarkable. Not a change of values, but of attitudes. . . ." *Children of the Mire*, pp. 96–97.

[7] With specific reference to this aspect of the poetry of the Cuban writer, see my article "Naturaleza y metáfora en algunos poemas de José Martí," *Temas del modernismo hispánico y otros estudios* (Madrid, 1974), pp. 241–260.

[8] When Paz discusses the changes introduced into poetry by the postmodernistas *(Children of the Mire*, p. 97), he also defines to some extent the nature of the modern poem, reworking and reducing an earlier and a more explicit text devoted to the description of the poem as conceived by Laforgue, Lugones and López Velarde ("The Road of Passion," *The Siren and the Seashell*, pp. 71–73).

central always to Paz's thesis:

> The aesthetic of change is no less illusory than that
> of imitation of the Ancients. One tends to minimize,
> changes, the other to exaggerate them. The history of the
> poetic revolutions of the modern age has been none other
> than the dialogue between analogy and irony. The for-
> mer rejected the modern age; the latter, analogy. Modern
> poetry has been criticism of the modern world and criti-
> cism of itself. . . . (p. 161)

As the author himself clearly states in the short preface to
Children of the Mire (p. vii), these final pages dealing primarily
with poetry since the time of the avant-garde are closely related to the manifesto of 1965 ("Los signos en rotación"),
published now as a second and different epilogue to the latest
edition of *El arco y la lira* (1967, pp. 253–284). He further
implies that his book of 1974 is a continuation and amplifica-
tion of certain questions posed in *El arco y la lira* which first
appeared in 1956, with specific reference to the problem of
poetic communication (p. v). Once again Paz insists that irre-
spective of linguistic and cultural differences there is only one
modern poetry in our Western world (p. vi). Such unity is
shown through the study of relevant historical movements in
poetry. The modern poets, from Romanticism on, discover in
their rejection of rationalism the tradition of analogy and en-
visage the world as a vast series of correspondences. However,
as we have seen, for the romantic and symbolist writer it is
irony that subverted this comfortable system, and one aspect
of the complex dialogue within the poem is precisely this contradictory relationship which exists between analogy and irony.

I preferred to use in my title for these general remarks on
Octavio Paz the word *tribute* instead of *debt* because the latter
seemed at the time somewhat too personal. Nevertheless, I
still hope that my modest understanding of modern poetry has
been made richer and enhanced in virtue of what I hope to
have learned from the instructive Paz texts read with admiration
and affection over the past years. May I be permitted, then,
in closing to candidly confess my debt and gratitude to him?
I owe a great deal to Octavio Paz: to his intellectual and human
example. Without hesitation I once more reaffirm this debt.

☆   ☆   ☆

Julio Ortega

NOTES ON PAZ

1

Octavio Paz is one of the major writers of Latin America.
Like César Vallejo, he has sought to give poetry a meaning
which can respond to the disarticulation of Western culture.
But if Vallejo believed that that meaning lay in solidarity with
rebellions throughout the world because a different history
seemed possible, Paz believes that poetic meaning is a communion of humanity and of its latent capacities to liberate
language in a world pervaded by the repressive forms of East
and West. Like Borges, Paz quickly understood the peculiar-
ity of Hispano-American culture lay in its openness, its dramatic merging of seemingly dissimilar origins. Unlike Borges,
Paz believes cultures are not simply speculative forms or equivalent models of perception; rather he criticizes these cultural
models (beginning with the Mexican) in his search of an original, revealing idea. Thus Borges' China is a paradox of knowledge and its hermeneutics; Paz's India, a source of generating
and regenerating consciousness. If in Borges, skepticism and
surprise relinquish language to the imagination, in Paz plenitude
and the instant hope for a reintegration from language. On
the other hand, Paz is closer to Julio Cortázar and José Lezama Lima, his strict contemporaries. Like Cortázar, Paz has
explored a series of alternating discourses: Romantic Symbolism (Nerval, Novalis), Surrealism (and Duchamp's concept
of the critical work), Tantric Hinduism, the mythical and critical adventure of Mallarmé, spatial poetry and, finally, the
beginning and end of the avant-garde. This exploration reveals
Paz's intellectual curiosity, his permeability and his capacity
to respond. His work illustrates that renewed encounter and
discussion with the great currents of thought and contemporary art. In that exploration he has stated clearly his own concept of modern (or rather, post modern) art and the artist:
art as a space of renewal in a world without hope; the artist
as critic of language and responsible for that authentic space
of recognition. Like Lezama Lima, Paz has made from poetry
a self-sufficient space, non-explicit, an act of ritual representation and liberating desire.

2

Paz is a fortunate poet. He was in various places at the best possible time. In his youth he was in Spain together with other poets and writers who supported the Republican cause, but was too young for the traumatic experience of the Republic's defeat to have affected his literary and intellectual integrity—as it did so many others. He was in Paris between 1940 and 1950 where he was friends with Breton and Peret and where his poetry succeeded in freeing itself from "purist" and Symbolist diction and transformed itself, assimilating from Surrealism its expressive openness and poetic independence. During the 1960s he was Mexican Ambassador to India where his study of Tantric Buddhism enriched his thought and the concentration of his poetry. In 1969, in protest over the slaughter of students in Tlatelolco Plaza, Paz resigned his post and obtained, together with his political independence, in the seventies, an intellectual authority rarely seen in the Hispanic cultural world permitting him to make *Plural* the best Latin American review of the decade. Paz became a visible voice from Mexico against the authoritarianisms of the left and right. Even if it is easy to disagree with some of his views on certain matters, his dramatic independence, critical will and libertarian attitude are undeniable. Today he is one of the most stimulating writers of international literature: a writer who, following Surrealism and Modernism, has created a critical and poetic language animated simultaneously by an energy of change and the desire to maintain in the poetic world a place for dialogue. Paz must be one of the last poets with this radical faith in poetry as change and persistence: a faith not in the world, but in the word that criticizes and restores the world. Poetry is the final identity of the contemporary subject, the modern victim. Myth of language, poetry is the alternative: the subject reconstructed.

3

In Octavio Paz's work there are many memorable poems, but above all there are two grand moments: *La estación violenta (The Violent Season,* 1958) and *Blanco* (1967)—two very accomplished books where an exploration grows and culminates, radicalized by extreme freedom and precision.

From these poems a similar openness and concentration: the origin, the renewal of names, is in both works presented as a reconstruction, that is, through the mythical reencounter of an integrated form, prior to names. The first book breaks with Surrealist poetry—transforming it. Paz turns the figurative technique of Surrealism into the foundation of a rhythmic contrapuntal song, almost the intonation of a hymn, with long verses of dramatic and celebratory modulation. The expressive fullness of these poems is extraordinary. Among them, *Piedra de sol,* composed of eleven syllable verses, unites the Hispanic tradition of that meter with Aztec mythology and modern poetic reflection. Eros, poetry and the natural and historical world merge into a single song of liberation. *Blanco,* starting from a Mallarméan experience of poetic space as a "cosmic" renewal of the word, is a long poem about poetry and poetic knowledge. Space, sign, sound, verse, sequences, plots of sequences, are an analogical text where the substance of the world is a verbal substance, united by the mythical act to name and reconstitute. *Blanco* is also the reader's poem: to read it is to create it. To read, in other words, is to return here to the blank space where words will produce change and permanence, the instant and plenitude, criticism and conjunction. That is, after all, the promise of poetry: from that tradition Paz says it once again, in the beginning and in the renewing of names.

4

BORGES: The book and the fiction of reading ourselves.
PAZ: The poem and the drama of re-creating ourselves.
VALLEJO: The word as speech of subverted meaning.
PAZ: The word as a sign of a promised encounter.
NERUDA: Language as the sensuousness of the intelligible world.
PAZ: Language as the intelligence of the sensible world.
CORTÁZAR: Speech as the substance of which we are made.
PAZ: Speech as the space in which we are unpredictable.
LEZAMA LIMA: The image as the generating source of knowing.
PAZ: The image as a resistant instant of changing knowledge.

trans. from the Spanish by Kosrof Chantikian

☆   ☆   ☆

125

Jaime Alazraki

OCTAVIO PAZ–POETRY AS CODED SILENCE

For Octavio Paz modern poetry is criticism: "Since
Une saison en enfer," he has written, "our great poets have
made out of the negation of poetry the highest form of
poetry: their poems are criticism of the poetic experience, of
language and meaning, of the poem itself. The poetic word is
sustained by the negation of the word."[1] This theme embraces
much of Paz's own poetry, and silence, which accompanies
this criticism of the word as a poetic theme and as a discursive
meditation, is a sort of isobar which runs through the length
of his entire work. It is not an isolated theme, but a long reflection spreading throughout his oeuvre. Furthermore, this
reflection itself, in prose or in verse, is undertaken so that
silence and its underlying meanings may be evoked. Such is
the task of the poet: "Enamored of silence, the poet has no
choice but to speak" (*CA*, 74). In Paz this theme is a manifold
image. Stated in its most elementary meaning, silence is the
state before the word, the seminal point of the poem, the
empty space which precedes writing: "The image is a desperate device against the silence which invades us each time we
try to express the terrible experience of that which surrounds
us. The poem is language in tension: in the extreme of being
and in being up to the extreme. Extremes of the word and
extreme words, turned in upon their own entrails, showing
the reverse of speech: silence and non-meaning" (*AL*, 111).

Here his understanding of silence does not differ from
the rather limited definition of Max Picard: "Not until speech
comes out of silence does silence come out of pre-creation
into creation, out of the prehistoric into the history of man,

---

[1] Octavio Paz, *El arco y la lira* (Mexico, 2nd ed., 1967), p. 257. Paz's
works will be abbreviated as follows: *AL (El arco y la lira); CA (Corriente alterna*, Mexico, 1967); *LBP (Libertad bajo palabra*, Mexico, 2nd
ed., 1968); *S (Salamandra*, Mexico, 3rd ed., 1972); *LE (Ladera este*,
Mexico, 3rd ed., 1975); *PO (Las peras del olmo*, Barcelona, 2nd ed.,
1974); *SG (El Signo y el garabato*, Mexico, 1973); *CLS (Claude Lévi-
Strauss o el nuevo festín de Esopo*, Mexico, 1967); *MG (El mono gramático*, Barcelona, 1974); *HL (Los hijos del limo*, Barcelona, 2nd ed.,
1974).

into close relationship with man, becoming part of man and a lawful part of speech. But speech is more than silence, because truth is first expressed concretely by speech, not by silence."[2] Silence then, understood as a negative dimension: as non-meaning, as an opening toward the word, as the margin of the poem:

> El mundo cede y se desploma
> como metal al fuego.
> Entre mis ruinas me levanto,
> solo, desnudo, despojado,
> sobre la roca inmensa del silencio,
> como un solitario combatiente
> contra invisibles huestes
>
> (*LBP*, 90)

> (The world gives way and collapses
> like metal in fire.
> In the midst of my ruins I rise up
> alone, naked, forsaken
> on this vast rock of silence
> like a solitary fighter
> against invisible armies).

The poetic act is a struggle against silence and the poet seeks to overcome it with words: "By a path which in its own way, is negative, the poet reaches the edge of language. And this edge is called silence, blank page. A silence which is like a lake, a smooth and compact surface. Down below, submerged, words wait. And one must descend, go to the bottom, be quiet, wait. Sterility precedes inspiration, as emptiness precedes plenitude. The poetic word springs up after ages of drought" (*AL*, 147–48):

> Dios mudo, que al silencio del hombre que pregunta
>   contestas
>   sólo con silencio que ahoga
>
> (*LBP*, 94)

---

[2] Max Picard, *The World of Silence* (Chicago, 1952), p. 28.

(Mute God, who to humanity's questioning silence you
     answer
  only with a suffocating silence).

> El hombre está habitado por silencio y vacío.
> ¿Cómo saciar esta hambre
> cómo acallar y poblar su vacío?
>
> (*LBP*, 109)

(Humankind is haunted by silence and emptiness.
How to satisfy this hunger,
How to ease and fill this emptiness?)

And especially in "Visitas" (Visitors) from *El girasol (Sunflower)* and in "El sitiado" (The Besieged) from *¿Águila o sol?
(Eagle or Sun?):*

> Del silencio brota un árbol de música.
> Del árbol cuelgan todas las palabras hermosas,
> que brillan, maduran, caen.
>
> (*LBP*, 117)

(From silence sprouts a tree of music.
From this tree hangs every beautiful word,
which shines, ripens, falls).

> A mi derecha no hay nada. El silencio y la soledad
> extienden sus llanuras. ¡Oh mundo por poblar, hoja en
> blanco!
>
> (*LBP*, 203)

(To my right there is nothing. Silence and solitude
spread out their plains. Oh, world to fill, blank leaf!)

But this meaning of silence as prelude to the word, as
emptiness the poet must fill, already alternates from the beginning of his work with a conflicting notion: "Silence itself,"
Paz says in *The Bow and the Lyre,* "is inhabited by signs." In
his work there appear simultaneously two very different faces
of poetry: an almost absolute faith in the word—"The word is
humankind itself. We are made of words. They are our only

reality or at least, the only testimony of our reality. We cannot escape from language" (*AL*, 30–31), and an equally absolute suspicion of the word—"Poetic activity is born of desperation in the face of the impotence of the word and culminates in the recognition of the omnipotence of silence" (*CA*, 74). In a way, Paz's work summarizes these two moments in the history of European poetry: from the absolute sovereignty of the word to its impotence and sterility. Paz finds an answer to this apparent conflict between word and silence in Eastern thought:

> The Western world is the world of "this or that"; the Eastern, of "this and that" and even of "this is that." In the most ancient Upanishad the principle of the identity of contraries is clearly asserted: "You are woman. You are man. You are boy and also girl . . ." Taoism shows the same tendencies. . . . Chuang Tzu explains the functional and relative character of contraries in this way: "There is nothing that is not this; there is nothing that is not that. Such is the doctrine of the interdependence of this and that. Life is life in relation to death. And vice versa. Affirmation is affirmation in relation to negation. And vice versa. Therefore, if one leans on this, it would have to deny that. But this possesses its affirmation and its negation and also engenders its this and its that. So the true sage puts aside the this and the that and takes refuge in Tao."
>
> (*AL*, 102–3).

In the same chapter of *The Bow and the Lyre,* Paz quotes the *Tao Te Ching:* "The Tao that can be named / is not the eternal Tao; / The Name that can be said / is not the eternal Name"—and comments: "The condemnation of words stems from the inability of language to transcend the world of relative and interdependent contraries, of the this in relation to the that . . . All knowledge would then be reduced to knowing knowledge is impossible. Again and again the texts of Eastern tradition delight in this kind of ambiguity. The doctrine is resolved into silence." (*AL*, 104–5). And further on: "The same thing happens in Zen Buddhism, a doctrine which is resolved in paradox and silence." Nevertheless, that worship of silence in Eastern thought (the god of the *Svetasvatara Upanishad* governs the works of silence and reveals its radiant beauty and perfection in the harmony of silence) has been transmitted through images and texts, through a language which makes from the negation of language its most powerful word. A language which nears poetry and in whose paradoxical reality Paz finds a road for his Poetry: "Chuang Tzu says that the sage 'preaches the doctrine without words.' . . . The wordless preaching to which the Chinese Philosopher alludes is not that of example but of a language which is something more than language: word which says the unsayable. Although Chuang Tzu never thought of poetry as a language capable of transcending the meaning of this and that and saying the unsayable, his reasoning cannot be separated from images, word games and other poetic forms. Poetry and thought are interwoven in Chuang Tzu to form a single fabric, a single unique material . . . The same must be said of other doctrines. Thanks to the poetic image, Taoist, Hindu and Buddhist thought becomes comprehensible" (*AL*, 105–6). Paz refers to a language such that through it language is transcended in order to become presence, incommunicable image, spoken silence. Or as he puts it: A language in which "names and things fuse and are the same: poetry, realm where naming is being. The image says the unsayable. We must return to language in order to see how the image can say that which language, by its very nature, seems incapable of saying" (*AL*, 106).

From his earliest poems Paz searches for a language in which "naming is being," a language which takes refuge in silence and from its transparency rediscovers the world:

> Tengo que hablaros de ella:
> de un metal encondido,
> de una hierba sedienta,
> del silencio compacto de un arbusto;
> del ímpetu invisible
> que hace crecer las cosas,
> de lo que sólo vive
> como sangre y aliento.
> Del silencio del mundo,
> del tumulto del mundo.
> (*LBP*, 19)

(I must speak of her
of a hidden metal,
of a parched grass,
of the dense silence of a shrub;
of the invisible impulse
which makes things grow,
of that which only lives
like blood and breath.
Of the world's silence,
Of the world's uproar.)

The encounter with the Word is the encounter with silence—"[un] canto/cantando en el silencio deslumbrado" (a
song/sung in dazzling silence)—which from its nothingness
says "la plenitud de lo vivo" (the fullness of living):

Canta, desde su sombra
—y más, desde su nada—el alma.
Desnudo de su nombre canta el ser,
en el hechizo de existir suspenso,
de su propio cantar enamorado.
. . .
Es el secreto mediodía.
El alma canta, cara al cielo,
y sueña en otro canto,
sólo vibrante luz,
plenitud silenciosa de lo vivo.
(*LBP,* 39)

(The soul, from its shadow
—and even from its nothingness—sings.
Stripped of its name, the being sings,
in the spell of suspended existence,
of its own enamored song
. . .
It is the hidden afternoon.
The soul sings, facing the sky,
and dreams of another song,

vibrant light,
silent fullness of living.)

For Paz silence and plenitude coalesce and from this fusion the word emerges as a footprint of silence. Poetry does not dwell in words from which the poem is made, but in that space carved by words: "brota del fondo del silencio / otro silencio" (*LBP,* 42) (from the depths of silence springs / another silence). In his essay on the haiku, Paz discusses some examples from Yamazaki Sokan (1465–1553) and compares the original haiku: "Summer moon / if you put a handle on it / a fan!" with Antonio Machado's paraphrase in *Nuevas canciones (New Songs):* "A una japonesa / le dijo Sokan: / con la luna blanca / te abanicarás, / con la luna blanca / a orillas del mar" (To a Japanese woman / Sokan said: / with the white moon / you will fan yourself / with the white moon / at the seashore), and adds: "In spite of the fact that one of his virtues was innuendo, in this case Machado did not resist the very Hispanic and Hispanic American tendency for explication and reiteration. In his paraphrase the suggestion has disappeared, that part of the poem *not said* in which poetry truly lies" (*SG,* 118). Perhaps this footnote, as a marginal commentary, is the most precise description of the meaning of poetry as a search in the meanders and spaces of silence. The first poems of *Libertad bajo palabra (Liberty on Parole)* exalt this silence, which is sometimes confused with a hermeticism through which modern poetry, and in particular French poetry, attempts to grasp the ungraspable, to express a signified which escapes the signifiers of language. In Paz, this search is a dialogue with silence from the very beginning of his poetic work, a path leading from "one silence to another": "desembocamos al silencio / en donde los silencios enmudecen" (we flow into silence / where silence says nothing) states the last line of "Silencio" in *Condición de nube (Cloud Condition,* 1944). At this stage of his poetry, the theme still appears as the first formulation of a true poetic of silence, as a program his later work will fully carry through:

¿Cómo decir los nombres, las estrellas,
los albos pájaros de los pianos nocturnos
y el obelisco del silencio?

132

. . .

¿Cómo decir, camelia,
la menos flor entre las flores,
Cómo decir tus blancas geometrías?

¿Cómo decir, oh Sueño, tu silencio en voces?
(*LBP*, 53)

(How to speak of these names, these stars,
the white birds of evening pianos
and the obelisk of silence?
. . .
How to say camellia,
the least flower among flowers,
how to say your geometries of whiteness?

How to speak of, oh Dream, your silence in voices?)

Words are not an alternative to silence for Paz, but a transgression against words themselves. "It is not about the destruction of language, but an operation aimed at revealing the reverse of language, the other side of signs" (*SG*, 27–28). This idea appears formulated with still greater clarity in his essay on Tantric art: "The sign, whatever it may be, has the property of taking us beyond, always beyond. A perpetual *toward* . . . that is never a here. What writing says is beyond the written, and what Tantric painting presents is not in it. Where the poem ends, poetry begins; the presence is not the painted signs we see, but that which the signs invoke" (*SG*, 51). That *toward* . . . and that *beyond the written* is a space in whose boundaries the poem is resolved in the wake which words leave: a silence, yes, but different from that which precedes writing. The first is an empty space, amorphous, a void; the second is also a void, but full of suggestions: an empty space clipped by words which communicates from its invisible substance. The silence which precedes the poem is a sterile chaos; the silence which the poem depicts is a hole peopled by inaudible voices which, in the final analysis, are the true voices of poetry. "Piedra nativa" (Native Stone) traces this distance between the two silences:

Como las piedras del Principio
Como el principio de la Piedra
Como al Principio piedra contra piedra
Los fastos de la noche:
El poema todavía sin rostro
El bosque todavía sin árboles
Los cantos todavía sin nombre

Mas ya la luz irrumpe con pasos de leopardo
Y la palabra se levanta ondula cae
Y es una larga herida y un silencio sin mácula.

(LBP, 128)

(Like stones from the Beginning
Like the beginning of Stone
Like stone against stone at the Beginning
The chronicles of the night:
Poem without a face yet
Forest without trees yet
Songs without names yet

But the light now bursts with leopard steps
And the word rises quivers falls
And is a long wound and a flawless silence).

Even more explicitly, the prose poem "Trabajos del poeta" (Works of the Poet) confronts these two silences and attempts to describe the "paletadas del silencio cayendo en el silencio" (*LBP*, 149) (the strokes of silence falling into silence). A good number of the poems which follow, in *Libertad bajo palabra*, are an effort to hear this silence which the poem inscribes on words. "El río" (The River), for example, opens long "galleries" of reasoning: "un río de tinta" (a river of ink), "un discurso incomprensible y jadeante, un tartamudeo de aguas y piedras batallando, su historia" (an incomprehensible and panting speech, a stuttering of waters and battling stones, its history). This history is a "larga palabra que no acaba nunca" (long word which never ends): "Es una explanada desierta el poema, lo dicho no está dicho, lo no dicho es indecible" (The poem is a deserted esplanade, what has been said no longer

stands, what has not been said is unsayable). The poem celebrates its own failure: "que las palabras depongan armas y
sea el poema una sola palabra entretejida, un resplandor implacable que avanza" (that words may lay down their arms
and the poem be a single intertwining word, a relentless splendor advancing), but this failure is the poem's major triumph
because this "long word which never ends" is like a watermark
in the poem ("voices of water," one of the poems in *Vuelta*
will say) which from silence names the unnameable:

> y sea todo como la llama que se esculpe y se hiela en la
>   roca de entrañas transparentes,
> duro fulgor resuelto ya en cristal y claridad pacífica.

> Y el río remonta su curso, repliega sus velas, recoge sus
>   imágenes y se interna en sí mismo.

> (*LBP*, 232)

> (and may everything be like a flame that sculpts itself
>   and freezes into the rock of transparent bowels
> harsh glow already firm in crystal and peaceful clarity

> And the river goes back upstream, folds its sails, picks
>   up its images and curls into itself).

In the final book of *Libertad bajo palabra—La estación
violenta (The Violent Season)—*"Himno entre ruinas" (Hymn
Among the Ruins), the first poem, asks: "dónde desenterrar
la palabra" (where are we to unearth the word?); the next to
the last poem of this collection, "El cántaro roto" (The Broken Pitcher) tries to answer. It is an answer that goes back
"hacia atrás, hacia la fuente, . . . siglos arriba / más allá de la
infancia, más allá del comienzo, más allá de las aguas del
bautismo" (backwards, toward the source, . . . centuries up-
stream / beyond childhood, beyond the beginning, beyond
the baptismal waters), and toward the end urges: *hay que
desenterrar la palabra perdida (we must unearth the lost word).*
But between this assertion and the question the poem runs
like the imminence of an absent word, like a word incarnated
in that silence which for Paz has more and more become the

residence of poetry. This lost word does not appear in the poem as a physical presence because it is more than the sum of its words—it is what preceeded the words—but without naming it the poem names it, or at least it names one of its many faces.

In *Piedra de sol (Sun Stone)* this word is all words, "todos los nombres son un solo nombre" (all names are one name), a word which does not come to an end, like the poem itself which through the last six lines repeating the first six and together with the final colon suggest a circular reading of the poem. But in addition, this silence which leaves the poem unfinished is an invitation to the poetry inscribed in the poem. The poem continues in the reader. It is not a circle closing on itself, but a spiral which opens up. In "Fable" Paz intuits a "palabra inmensa / como un sol" (word as large / as a sun), a primeval word which contains all words. *Piedra de sol* is this word which speaks from the silence that confronts the reader. Word-silence which neither comments on nor summarizes itself. Not because of its extension (the poem) or the cosmic scope of its theme, but because the poetic experience lies in that encounter between the silence that comes after the reading of the poem and the silence of the reader. The one penetrates the other: one fertilizes the other, and from this fusion (a dialogue similar to lovemaking) emerges a meaning present neither in language nor even in the text of the poem. An experience which comes close to an illumination because the poem, when it hits its target, attains the impossible, blending language and silence, consciousness and innocence, reality and unreality: "Poetic illumination . . . consists of returning to the silence from which the poem began, only now weighed down with meaning" (*PO,* 130). Paz alludes to this silence when he asks toward the end of *Piedra de sol:*

> . . . y el silencio
> que se cubre de signos, el silencio
> que dice sin decir, ¿no dice nada?,
> ¿no son nada los gritos de los hombres?
> (*LBP,* 251)

> (. . . and the silence
> which covers itself with signs, the silence
> which says without saying, does it say nothing?
> Are the cries of humanity nothing?)

Throughout the poem this silence curdles in images—words that are miniatures of the word, tiny mirrors where the poem folds over its own image—but the notion they convey escapes our cognition. If what "we really know is not reality, but that part of reality which can be reduced to language and concepts" (*PO*, 95), poetic knowledge coins its own language by means of images and through them it can free itself from the tyranny of words and transcend them:

> escritura del mar sobre el basalto,
> escritura del viento en el desierto
> testamento del sol, granada, espiga.
> (*LBP*, 241)

> (writing of the sea on basalt,
> writing of the wind in the desert,
> testament of the sun, pomegranate, ear of corn.)

They are images of woman, indeed, but also images of the world, in the same way that the lines which follow—"todos los nombres son un solo nombre, / todos los rostros son un solo rostro, / todos los siglos son un solo instante" (all names are one name, / all faces a single face, / all centuries an instant) —are a cry for "our lost unity" and also images that offend scandalously the common sense of our consciousness, that disrupt the order and precisions set by logic to leave us facing a timeless time and an extraterritorial territory. What poetry proposes is no different than what Buddhism seeks: "The end of relations, the abolition of dialectics—a silence that is not the dissolution of language, but its *resolution*" (*CA*, 73). For Paz religion and poetry are separated by a thin wall. He has written extensively on this theme in *The Bow and the Lyre* and more recently in *Los hijos del limo (Children of the Mire)*: "Shelly's atheism is a religious passion . . . In the Middle Ages poetry was the servant of religion; but in the Romantic Age, it is the true religion, the fountainhead of the

137

Holy Scriptures. . . . And because poetry remains we can continue to read the Vedas and Bibles, not as religious but as poetic texts. . . . 'The Religions of all Nations are derived from each Nation's different reception of the Poetic Genius.'" (*HL,* 70, 78, 84). Nevertheless, there is a difference between mysticism and poetry, though that difference may be the fulcrum common to both: at the end of the religious text God awaits as a revelation that the Psalm or the Veda brings forth; at the end of the poetic text a silence awaits like an "imminence of a revelation which does not occur."[3] The religious text rests on the certainty of faith; the poetic text makes its faith out of uncertainty; religion is surrender, poetry, rapture; "Mysticism is an immersion in the absolute; poetry is an expression of the absolute or of the rupturing attempt to reach it" (*PO,* 99).

After *Libertad bajo palabra,* a good part of Octavio Paz's poetry is an exploration through a timeless time and through a territory without space in which the geography of silence is found. In *Salamandra* that effort to define the indefinable and to touch silence continues through new stations of the same journey—stopovers that bring us nearer to the sought destination, ascents through "thought which becomes rusty / and gangrenous writing" toward "the silence of the sun" from which the Word glows:

> Los nombres no son nombres
> No dicen lo que dicen
> Yo he de decir lo que no dicen
> Yo he de decir lo que dicen.
> (*S,* 13)

> (Names are not names
> They do not say what they say
> I will say what they do not say
> I will say what they say).

In the poem dedicated to Cernuda, Paz returns to the notion that reading a poem is a creative (or re-creative) ex-

---

[3] Jorge Luis Borges, *Otras inquisiciones* (Buenos Aires, 1964), p. 12.

ercise in which the poem and the reader exchange their silences in a symbiotic act from whose alchemy true poetry is born:

> Con letra clara el poeta escribe
> Sus verdades oscuras
> > Sus palabras
> No son un monumento público
> Ni la Guía del camino recto
> Nacieron del silencio
> Se abren sobre tallos de silencio
> Las contemplamos en silencio
> Verdad y error
> > Una sola verdad
> Realidad y deseo
> > Una sola substancia
> Resuelta en manantial de transparencias
> > > (S, 28)

> (With clear handwriting the Poet writes
> His obscure truths
> > His words
> Are not a public monument
> Nor Guide to the true way
> Born out of silence
> They open up on stems of silence
> We contemplate them in silence
> Truth and error
> > A single truth
> Reality and desire
> > A single substance
> Resolved into a fountain of transparencies).

The next two poems—"La palabra escrita" (The word written) and "La palabra dicha" (The word spoken)—are new meditations concerning the problem of the word. The last two lines of "The word spoken" present a very tight synthesis of two central notions of Paz's poetic thought: the vision of poetry as a return from the language of science to the

139

language of innocence—"olvidar lo que sabemos" (to forget what we know)—and the conception of silence as the firmest territory of the word ("thought of smoke"):

> Inocencia y no ciencia:
> Para hablar aprende a callar.
> (S, 32)

> (Innocence and not science
> To speak learn to keep quiet).

One can understand that to Vasconcelos' warnings in "The Same Time" ("Dedicate yourself to philosophy") and to Ortega y Gasset's advice ("Learn German / And begin to think"), Paz would reply: "Un día sabré menos y abriré los ojos" (One day I will know less and open my eyes) and especially "Yo no escribo para matar al tiempo / Ni para revivirlo / Escribo para que me viva" (S, 43) (I do not write to kill time / Nor to relive it / I write so that it will live me).

In another poem, "Noche en claro" (Clear night), the poem is "gateway" and "bridge" and a river flowing by the other shore: "el río de los siglos, el río de los signos, el río de los astros" (the river of centuries, the river of signs, the river of stars) and between this constellation of signs flows the "escritura silencio que canta" (writing—silence which sings). Woman is an image of the world, or rather, woman is the world which in turn is the song through which poetry resolves itself into silence:

> . . .
> Pero tu sexo es innombrable
> La otra cara del ser
> La otra cara del tiempo
> El revés de la vida
> Aquí cesa todo discurso
> Aquí la belleza no es legible
> Aquí la presencia se vuelve terrible
> Replegada en sí misma la Presencia es vacío
> Lo visible es invisible
> Aquí se hace visible lo invisible

140

Aquí la estrella es negra
La luz es sombra luz la sombra
Aquí el tiempo se para
Los cuatro puntos cardinales se tocan
Es el lugar solitario el lugar de la cita
                        (S, 63–64)

(. . .
But your sex is unnameable
The other face of being
The other face of time
The other side of life
All talk stops here
Beauty is no longer legible
Presence becomes terrifying
Fallen back on itself Presence is emptiness
The visible is invisible
Here the invisible is made visible
Here the star is black
Light is shadow light shadow
Time stops here
The four cardinal points touch
It is the secluded place the place of rendezvous).

The dominant theme of *Salamandra* is woman and the
mystery of love. But woman is the natural world recovered,
and love, the path of return to that world, buried by the
mechanics of life and chattering: "We moderns, incapable of
innocence, born in a society that makes us naturally artificial
and that has stripped us of our human value in order to convert us into commodities, search vainly for lost humanity, for
innocent humanity. All serious attempts of our culture, from
the end of the eighteenth century, are directed toward recov-
ering it, to dreaming it" (*PO*, 104–5). Paz has said that in his
adolescence the reading of Breton's *L'amour fou* and Blake's
The Marriage of Heaven and Hell opened the doors of modern
poetry for him like "an art of love" that later "life and the
East have corroborated": the beloved woman as the way
which leads to that time of innocence and human value; "the
analogy, or rather, the identity between the loved one and

141

nature." "The couple is time recaptured, time before time . . .
Woman is a bridge, place of reconciliation between the natural
and human worlds. She is language taking shape, revelation
incarnate" (*CA*, 58-59). Poetry emerges thus as a dialogue
between the tangible language of the loved woman and the
signs of the poem's language:

> Te hablaré un lenguaje de piedra
> (Respondes con un monosílabo verde)
> Te hablaré un lenguaje de nieve
> (Respondes con un abanico de abejas)
> Te hablaré un lenguaje de agua
> (Respondes con una canoa de relámpagos)
> Te hablaré un lenguaje de sangre
> (Respondes con una torre de pájaros)
>
> (*S*, 78)

> (I will speak to you in a language of stone
> [You reply with a green syllable]
> I will speak to you in a language of snow
> [You reply with a fan of bees]
> I will speak to you in a language of water
> [You reply with a canoe of lightning]
> I will speak to you in a language of blood
> [You reply with a tower of birds]).

The language of the poet—stone, snow, water, blood—
stirs up a multitude of suggestions, but the attribute common
to these four images is their condition of silence. There is a
clear opposition between the sobriety of these substances (in
their solid colors and in their restrained movement) and the
exuberance of the images of the woman's language (intense
and mottled colors, rapid and lively movements). In the poet's
language there are elementary materials; in the language of
woman there are creatures (birds, bees) and elementary phenomena (lightning, greenness). The first language lives in its
silence; the second is inhabited by a song. The two, however,
evoke and invoke a natural world in which human consciousness is absent except in the text itself that inscribes the poem.
The poem, whose theme is an intertwining of two languages

142

in whose dialogue love speaks, is also "articulation of the duality consciousness/innocence" in whose synthesis Paz sees the final mission of poetry.[4] The poem which began as a dialogue between man and woman reunited in love ends as a dialogue between that primordial world of nature (innocence) and that artificial world of consciousness (language) reunited in the poem. Words mute, silence speaks. Love whose nature is silence ascends to the text of the poem. The text crystallizes silence. This magic is called poetry.

But it is in *Ladera este* where the perception of this theme reaches its fullest moment, and the questions set forth throughout his entire work are resolved in three of the most lucid and concentrated poems of the collection: "Letter to León Felipe," "Reading John Cage" and *Blanco*. "Letter to León Felipe," besides being a live dialogue with the Spanish Poet, is a reformulation of some of the concerns and quests of poetry. Paz opposes two green stains—"two parrots in full flight"—to language: a way of confronting metonymically the natural world with the artifices of culture, the innocence which the poet seeks and language as his only road of return to which he is forced by his condition as a creature of words. From this challenge, language inevitably ends in defeat because between words and things there is an abyss that has exiled humanity from the natural world. Language, incapable of communication with the world of things, creates a universe of signs and comments on itself never endingly:

> No nos queda dijo Bataille
> Sino escribir comentarios
> > Insensatos
> Sobre la ausencia de sentido del escribir
> Comentarios que se borran
> > > (*LE*, 91)

> (Nothing remains for us said Bataille
> but to write foolish
> > Commentaries

---

[4] See especially the essay "Poesía de soledad y poesía de comunión," in *Las peras del olmo*. [English trans. in *The Siren and the Seashell*. —Ed.]

On the absence of meaning in writing
Commentaries that erase themselves).

Things ("two parrots in full flight") defy movement,
leap, fly; words, on the other hand, "dissipate themselves /
their movement / is a return to immobility." Poetry is "a
senseless undertaking" because it proposes to construct with
language, which has created a breach between the natural
world and humanity, a bridge of return to that world; it is
madness because the poet asks immobility (language) to become movement. Modern poetry turns into a religion when
it assumes the miracles denied to religion by the omnipotence
(or rather arrogance) of the sciences. Its devotion to the word
requires a faith in the (poetic) word greater perhaps than that
which the pantheon of any religion required from its believers.
If language represents the historic fall that separated humankind from its primordial world, it is understandable that the
poetic endeavor should begin as a criticism of language and
then proceed to rescue humankind from the traps of its own
spell:

La escritura poética

Es borrar lo escrito
Escribir
Sobre lo escrito
Lo no escrito

. . .

La escritura poética es
Aprender a leer
El hueco de la escritura
En la escritura
No huellas de lo que fuimos
Caminos
Hacia lo que somos
(LE, 91)

(To write poetry
Is to erase the written
To write
On the written

144

The unwritten

. . .
To write poetry is

Learning to read
The empty space of writing

In the writing
Not the footprints of what we were

Paths
Toward what we are).

If writing poetry is "to write on the written the unwritten" and "learning to read the empty space of writing," the poem is inexorably "the unwritten," "the empty space," all that language is not and will never be, but which poetry compels it to be. Without mentioning the word silence, Paz names it in the most convincing way: keeping it quiet. But we already know that for Paz silence is not the absence of the word: "The West teaches us that Being dissolves itself in meaning and the East that meaning dissolves itself in something that is neither Being nor non-Being: it is a Same which no language except silence designates. So humankind is made up in such a way that silence becomes also language" (*CLS*, 125). How to say this silence? If the poem is, in the end, "the unwritten," "the empty space of writing," and language at the same time, then Paz is really saying the poem does not have to be either this or that, but "this and that," writing and silence, writing which says silence and silence which is manifested through writing. Not without reason did poets begin speaking of poetry as verbal alchemy.

Finally: what does this silence reveal? Before becoming a concern to modern poetry, the meaning of silence was a question placed at the heart of Buddhist thought; Paz sums it up in *Claude Lévi-Strauss or the New Feast of Aesop:*

The word of Buddha has meaning, though it asserts that nothing has, because it aims at silence: if we wish to know what he really said, we ought to question his silence. Now, the interpretation of what Buddha *did not say* is the crux of the great controversy which has divided schools of Buddhism from the beginning. Tradition tells us the Enlightened One did not answer ten questions . . .

For some those questions could not be answered; for
others, Gautama did not know how to answer; and for
still others, he preferred not to answer. K. N. Jayatilleke
translates the interpretations of these schools into modern terms. If Buddha did not know the answers he was
a skeptic or a naive agnostic; if he preferred to remain
quiet because to answer might have kept his listeners
from the true way, he was a pragmatic reformer; if he
kept quiet because there was no possible answer, he was
an agnostic rationalist (the questions are beyond the
limits of reason) or a logical positivist (the questions
lack meaning and therefore, answers). The young Sin-
halese professor favors this last solution . . . But this
interpretation, not very far from Lévi-Strauss' position,
forgets another possibility: silence itself is an answer.

(*CLS*, 125–26)

What is not said is what is said: such is the answer that
"Reading John Cage" suggests. Although the long reflection
on silence in this poem alludes to music, the comments there
are equally applicable to poetry. Silence which constitutes a
response, silence which speaks, is not a wide barren plain of
language; language invents silence in the same way "music /
invents silence" and "architecture / invents space" and just as
"music is not silence" but "silence is music," neither is language silence and, on the other hand, silence is the most powerful language our language is capable of eliciting. *Silence is
an idea and is not an idea:* it is not an idea because in our logical thinking silence is a negation of ideas, but it is an idea because silence transmits *something,* though this *something*
lacks a conceptual referent: idea that ideas cannot express,
and which can only be conveyed through silence. *Silence is
the space of music* and this space is the environment where
music is made possible and where silence can generate its
idea. The language of poetry also creates a space: residence
and speech of silence. This space must not be confused with
the new format of the poem which since *Un Coup de Dés*
a good part of modern poetry has adopted, though that new
arrangement of space between lines far from being purely or-
namental or visual, has a definite function as an expressive
vehicle. More than the physical space of the poem, it deals

146

with the mental space which the poem opens in the reader:
empty space of writing which is perceived by the reader in
the act of reading as a silence generating the only meanings
denied to language:

No hay silencio

Salvo en la mente

(*LE*, 81)

(There is no silence

except in the mind).

Claude Lévi-Strauss and *Blanco* appeared in the same
year; essay and poem were written in 1966 in Delhi, India.
The last pages of the essay (125–28) can be read as a brief
meditation on silence; *Blanco,* or at least its central column,
"is a poem whose theme is the passage of the word, from one
silence to the next, passing through four stages: yellow, red,
green, and blue" (*LE*, 145). This poem represents the culmination of that search. Culmination and conclusion, since the
next book, *Vuelta* (1976), hardly mentions it. It is present as
context, but with *Blanco,* this long reflection which began
with Paz's first poems draws to a close. What *Blanco* suggests
is a meaning already anticipated partly in his discussion on
Lévi-Strauss and already found in a different form in *The Bow
and the Lyre:*

> Silence is in itself an answer. This was the interpreta-
> tion of the Madhyamika School and of Nagarjuna and
> his disciples of what Buddha *did not say.* There are two
> silences: one, before speech, is an attempt at meaning;
> another, after speech, is the knowledge that the only
> thing worth saying cannot be said. Buddha said every-
> thing which it is possible to say with words: the errors
> and achievements of reason, the truth and lies of the
> senses, the illumination and the void of the instant, the
> freedom and slavery of nihilism. Words filled with rea-
> sons that cancel themselves and of sensations that con-
> sume each other. *But his silence says something different.*
> (*CLS*, 127)

Language is, as Wittgenstein said, "a picture of the world," but of the world invented by human beings: an artificial world created by culture that has its cornerstone in language. If "reason is language" as Johann Georg Hamann said, it is through language that humankind knows the world, but knowledge, as Ernst Cassirer has observed, "can never reproduce the true nature of things as they are, but must frame their essence in 'concepts.' But what are concepts except formulations and creations of thought, which, instead of giving us the true forms of objects, show us rather the forms of thought itself? Consequently, all schemata which science evolves in order to classify, organize and summarize the phenomena of the real world turn out to be nothing but arbitrary schemes—airy fabrics of the mind which express not the nature of things, but the nature of mind. So knowledge has been reduced to a kind of fiction, to a fiction that recommends itself by its usefulness, but must not be measured by any strict standard of truth, if it is not to melt away into nothingness."[5] More briefly, Jung has warned that "Western reality is in danger of losing its shadow altogether, of identifying itself with its fictive personality and of identifying the world with the abstract picture painted by scientific rationalism."[6] But if, as Jung believes, we have become the slave of our own fiction and a purely conceptual world gradually replaces reality, how then can we return to reality if we are separated from it by a wall of symbols which represents the foundation of our culture? How can we relinquish this fiction which has made us into what we are, and with which we have constructed our world? Referring to contemporary science, a North American scientist said recently, perhaps with much reason: "We have created a kind of world from which we cannot return." Wittgenstein postulates in his *Philosophical Investigations* a thesis opposed to the one presented in his *Tractatus*: "Philosophy is a battle against the bewitchment of our intelligence by means of language," and adds: "The results of philosophy are the uncovering of one or another piece of plain nonsense and of bumps that the understanding has got by running its head up against the limits of language."[7] Philosophy has always been a kind

---

[5] Ernst Cassirer, *Language and Myth* (New York, 1953), pp. 7–8
[6] C. G. Jung, *The Undiscovered Self* (Boston, 1964), p. 82.
[7] Ludwig Wittgenstein, *Philosophical Investigations* (New York, 1968), 109, 119.

of X-ray of language, and consequently its limits and range are the limits and range of language; philosophical investigation moves on the tracks of language; if it abandoned those tracks, it would derail. It makes sense that Heidegger sought in Hölderlin, and poetry in general, the answers that his systems could not provide; his answer, one of his answers, is a line from Hölderlin: "Poetically man dwells."[8] Where philosophy ends, poetry begins. If language has bewitched our intelligence, poetry will try to bewitch language. Here *to bewitch* means to force language to keep quiet so that from its silence—a momentary silence carved in the substance of language as its space—may rise its deepest voice: a bridge of return toward true reality. The East was in love with silence: "When the mind is silent," the *Maitri Upanishad* says, "beyond weakness or non-concentration, then it can enter into a world which is far beyond the mind: the highest End." In that silence, the chaos of the world becomes harmony. The god of Brahmanism is "eternal silence and cannot be seen by the eye nor can words reveal it," but Brahman reveals itself through silence: "It can be seen indivisibly in the silence of contemplation."[9] To a certain extent, Paz's interest in Eastern thought lies in that cultivation of silence as the resolution of phenomenal reality (Samsara) and as the resolution of language itself. Toward the end of his essay on Lévi-Strauss, Paz says:

> Language is the kingdom of dialectics which ceaselessly destroys itself and is reborn only to die. Language is dialectics, operation, communication. If Buddha's silence were the expression of this relativism, it would not be silence, but word. This isn't so: with his silence, movement, operation, dialectics, word, all cease. At the same time, it is neither the negation of dialectics nor of movement: Buddha's silence is the *resolution* of language. We come out of silence and return to it: to the word that has stopped being word.
>
> (*CLS*, 127)

Thus "Nirvana is Samsara" but "Samsara is not Nirvana"

---

[8] In *Poetry, Language, Thought* (New York, 1971), pp. 213–29.
[9] *The Upanishads.* "Mundaka Upanishad." III.i.8.

and "silence is music" but "music is not silence": "Silence is
an idea / The fixed idea of music" (*LE*, 81). There is silence
before music—empty silence—but the true silence occurs after
music, in music, or as a resolution of music. Such is the silence poetic language seeks: a silence that poetry achieves
through the incantation of its word:

> el comienzo
>> el cimiento
> la simiente
>> latente
> la palabra en la punta de la lengua
> inaudita   inaudible
>> impar
> grávida   nula
>> sin edad
> la enterrada con los ojos abiertos
> inocente   promiscua
>> la palabra
> sin nombre   sin habla
>> (*LE*, 147)

> (the beginning
>> the source
> the seed
>> latent
> word on the tip of the tongue
> unheard of   inaudible
>> odd
> gravid   void
>> ageless
> the woman buried with open eyes
> innocent   promiscuous
>> the word
> nameless   speechless).

The poetic word (silence) is "el lenguaje deshabitado,"
(uninhabited language), "sin nombre" (nameless) and "sin
habla" (speechless). The poem is a ladder of words that, upon

reaching silence, throws away the ladder and remains in that blank space which is not an absence of color, but the resolution of all colors. Like light, which integrates in its whiteness all colors, the second silence of poetry is not absence, but presence of words, though now integrated in the poem as the "resolution of language." The poem is an inverted prism which restores the myriad fragments in which language has been divided into that "one word, as large as a sun" which, like light, disappears into the transparency of its white silence.

Such an operation implies a sacrifice of language in whose ceremony—the poem—words atone until they are purified and melt away:

> El lenguaje
> Es una expiación,
> Propiciación
> Al que no habla,
> Emparedado
> Cada día
> Asesinado,
> El muerto innumerable.
> Hablar
> Mientras los otros trabajan
> Es pulir huesos,
> Aguzar
> Silencios
> Hasta la transparencia,
> Hasta la ondulación,
> El cabrilleo,
> Hasta el agua.
> (*LE*, 152–53)

> (Language
> Is expiation,
> Propitiation
> To whomever does not speak,
> Imprisoned
> Each day
> Assassinated,

The innumerable dead one.

> To speak

While others work
Is to polish bones,

> To sharpen

Silences

> Into transparency,

Into undulation,

> The rippling,

into water.)

The four states through which the central column of the poem travels, yellow, red, green and blue, point to a clarity—water—in which each singular color disappears in order to become transparent—"transparency is all that is left"—just as the "mujer tendida *hecha a la imagen del mundo*" (woman lying down *made in the image of the world*) is the world or rather, the world is the dispersion of woman, a bundle of overflowing images which in woman cluster in one image, a primordial world: "tu cuerpo son los cuerpos del instante" (your body is the bodies of the instant), "presente que no acaba" (never-ending present). But woman is also part of this fragmented world, she is in it as silence is in words, as a "bridge," as a "place of reconciliation between the natural and human worlds" (CA, 58–59); she is language and silence, silence which becomes language: "tú te repartes come el lenguaje *espacio dios descuartizado*" (LE, 162) (you divide yourself like language *space cut up god*). In his essay on Breton, Paz says: "Woman is concrete language, revelation incarnate: 'la femme n'est plus qu'un calice débordant de voyelles'" (CA, 59). Definition of woman which is at the same time a definition of poetry. Woman and poetry are for Paz different versions of the same silence full of meaning: poetry like woman "is a bridge, place of reconciliation between the natural and the human worlds."

Through the fiction of language, the poet seeks to recover the world's reality, and through love, reach his lost innocence: "entrar en mí / al entrar en tu cuerpo" (LE, 154) (to enter myself / on entering your body). Is it by chance that the two great themes of Paz's poetry should be love and language? Yet his erotic stand *is* also a poetic stand. Woman is dispersed in her body and only through love does she disappear to become "time before time"; her body, "lenguaje repartido" (dispersed language), dissolves into the fullness of silence, ceases to be dispersion and becomes harmony. Love, like the poetic act, begins in silence in order to reach another silence, begins on one shore to arrive at the other shore. Woman's body (and man's) is that language on which the poem rests to reach love (poetry). Love and poetry tear away the fiction of the world—human body dispersed in its functions, picture painted with words—in order to touch solid ground again. Departing from the unreality of language, poetry finds its way into reality: "La irrealidad de lo mirado / Da realidad a la mirada" (The unreality of the seen / Makes real the seeing). And what is the substance of that reality recovered by poetry? Isn't the poem but language, irrevocably language? The answer, from *Blanco*:

> El árbol de los nombres
> > Real irreal
> Son palabras
> > Aire son nada
> El habla
> > Irreal
> Da realidad al silencio
> > Callar
> Es un tejido de lenguaje
> > Silencio
> > (*LE,* 166–67)

> (The tree of names
> > Real unreal
> Are words
> > Air are nothing
> Speech
> > Unreal
> Gives reality to silence
> > Stillness
> Is a fabric of language
> > Silence).

153

What poetic language says is what it does not say: a silence that, like a love spasm, is nothing and everything, time in which the unreality of the world vanishes for an instant ("perpetual present") to leave us face to face with a primordial reality, a wholeness glimpsed like lightning, silence. Buddhism understood this silence with a lucidity rarely granted to the Western mind:

> What Buddha's silence says is neither negation nor affirmation. It says something else; it alludes to a beyond that is here. It says *Sunyata*: everything is empty because everything is full, the word is not a statement because the only statement is silence. Not nihilism but relativism which destroys itself and goes beyond itself. Movement is not resolved in immobility; it is immobility, and immobility is movement. The negation of the world implies a return to the world, asceticism is a return to the senses, Samsara is Nirvana, reality is the loving and terrifying cipher of the unreal, the instant is not a refutation, but the incarnation of eternity, the body is not a window to infinity: it is infinity itself . . . To reduce the world to meaning is as absurd as reducing it to the senses . . . Vibration, waves, signs and responses: silence. Not the knowledge of emptiness: an *empty knowledge.* The Buddha's silence is not knowledge but what comes after knowledge: wisdom. An unknowing.
>
> (CLS, 127–28)

Paz's work rises toward that "coded silence": a road that travels where "roads end." *Blanco* points toward that silence —where silence ends—with sibylline rhythm, like a text that speaks from its blank space loaded with meanings, from the reverse of the signs: not silence of language but language of silence.

Paz's work, like the fig tree of his poem, has "countless arms." It would be impossible (and preposterous) to attempt to trace one single line that defines it, but I think that this counterpoint between language and silence is the trunk from which his best poetry grows and branches out. We must only reexamine the pages of *El mono gramático* to realize to what degree Paz agonizes, like a seer, over that dialogue. The poet's plight is that of Sisyphus'. "There is no end, everything has been a perpetual rebeginning. What I say is a continuation of what I am going to say and which I never finish saying. In writing, I walk toward meaning; on reading what I write, I erase it, I dissolve the road. Each attempt ends in the same way: dissolution of the text in reading, expulsion of meaning by the written. The search for meaning culminates in the apparition of a reality that is beyond meaning and which disintegrates it, destroys it" (*MG,* 114–15). But the situation of the poet is also that of a visionary. If the text is dissolved in its reading, and if writing expels the meaning of the poem it is because poetry is a constant struggle between language and a meaning beyond language. In that strange struggle, the poet seeks to make language say what it cannot say. The poem is a testimony to that struggle, and that testimony speaks not through language but through space formed by the written text: "Poetic writing resolves itself in the abolition of the written: finally it confronts us with an inexpressible reality. The reality which poetry reveals and which appears behind language—that reality visible only through the cancellation of language in which the poetic operation consists—is literally unbearable and maddening. At the same time, neither humankind nor language are what they are without the vision of this reality. Poetry nourishes and destroys us, gives us speech and condemns us to silence" (*MG,* 113–14).

This silence *is* the most genuine voice of poetry because from it poetry communicates what language cannot say. Language is the "consequence (or the cause) of our exile from the universe, and it represents the gap between things and us. It is also our response to this gap. If that exile ceased, language would cease" (*MG,* 114). As long as this exile exists, as long as humankind remains banished by the unreality of language, as long as the world remains an invention of the spirit, the silence which poetry invites will keep being a road of access to the transparency of the world. And that transparency "is all that remains."

trans. from the Spanish by Kosrof Chantikian

☆　　　　　☆　　　　　☆

Kenneth Rexroth

A TRIBUTE

Octavio Paz is without any question the best Poet in the Western Hemisphere. There is no writer in English who can compare with him.

Jack Hirschman

THE INSIDE OF THE AVOCADO

Homage to Octavio Paz

"The word *paz*
written on
the inside of the avocado
    O Leonora
when I opened it
the word *paz*
written many times
    over
along with *revolution!*
O sister
through this cell
I read your message,
the words like paths
our liberty will
walk,
ciphers the cartography
of the end
of martyrdom,
all inside the avocado,
on the skin of
    the avocado
in the moonlight."

Homero Aridjis

THE POEM

to Octavio Paz

The poem turns above the head of a man
in circles now far-off now near

Discovering it he tries to possess it
but the poem disappears

With what he is able to grasp
he makes the poem

what escapes him
belongs to future men

trans. from the Spanish by Anthony Rudolf

Anthony Rudolf

OCTAVIO PAZ: AN INTERVIEW

Anthony Rudolf: A volume of your 'selected poems,' *Configurations,* . . . published by Jonathan Cape and one of . . . three books of yours . . . published in France by Gallimard is also a 'selected poems.' But the respective selections are not identical. Why is this?

Octavio Paz: I did not choose the poems myself. The poets who did the translations chose them, but in general I agree with their choice. The difference between the two selections is justifiable because some of my poems are closer to the French poetic tradition and naturally were translated into French, and similarly with the English book. I don't think the poet himself has the right to choose.

Both books contain 'recent' poems but I don't think one should speak of early or recent poems in the work of a poet. The first poems are already a premonition, and sometimes a refutation, of the last ones. Each book of mine is a prolongation, a critical prolongation. I *continue myself* in the text and watch myself disappear little by little. The poetic operation cannot be distinguished from the critical operation.

Rudolf: What you say about two traditions is interesting. Will you go into that more fully?

Paz: I believe that Western poetry is *one.* I believe profoundly in its unity. At the same time I believe in its plurality. The French tradition and the English tradition in this epoch are at opposite poles to each other. French poetry is more radical, more total. In an absolute and exemplary way it has assumed the heritage of European Romanticism, a romanticism which begins with William Blake and the German Romantics like Novalis, and via Baudelaire and the Symbolists culminates in twentieth century French poetry, notably Surrealism. It is a poetry where the world becomes writing and language becomes the double of the world. We find this admirably in Mallarmé. At the same time, as Bataille noticed, it is a poetry where the notion of transgression is of capital importance.

159

French poetry has lived this ambivalence between the world as writing and writing as a transgression against the world.

On the other hand, with regard to poetry written in English: the language had become detached from the European tradition, the central tradition, and Americans like Eliot, Pound and Stevens tried to return to it. Certainly English poetry, like all European poetry, is a Romantic poetry, but in the early part of this century it was at a loose end, adrift, until the Americans went to French and other European literature. French poetry has been a revolution. The achievement of Pound and Eliot was a *restoration,* a reestablishing of English within the mainstream. It is instructive to compare early Yeats with late Yeats.

Rudolf: You evoke Surrealism. After the War you participated in the Surrealist movement in France. Does Surrealism still have an active role for you? Does it still have any lessons for us? How does it relate to your later, Eastern influences?

Paz: To the extent that Surrealism is a school I think that it has been dead for a long time. But if we think of it as an attitude before the world, a disposition of the spirit, not a way of doing things but a way of being, then I don't think it's dead. What attracted me at first in it was its moral demands, also the idea that poetry is a criticism of itself and of society and of the world; and also of the poet. Surrealism has shown us that the notion of the author is perhaps illusory.

Surrealism, paradoxically, brought me close to the Oriental world. When I arrived in India (even before I went I was interested in the Oriental world, and in particular, Buddhism) I found certain similarities with Surrealism in the criticism of the world and the self, which is the essence of Buddhism. Naturally Surrealism like all Western thought attempts to change the world, whereas Buddhism tries to *nullify* it, to neutralize it. In my case the most important thing for me through Buddhism and Surrealism has been this neutralization of the self, not, I emphasize, of my personality. The notion of the self seems to me destined to perish.

Rudolf: What will replace the self? A notion of the other? An otherness? That heterogeneousness of which Bataille spoke?

Paz: On condition you know which other . . . No, because the 'other' too is a self. I think Bataille, like Surrealism, was bound and knew he was bound, to that dialectic of the self and the other, which is so Western. But what interests me (and it is for the same reason I find the thought of Lévi-Strauss so interesting) is the dissolution of the self. At that moment one finds not the other, but the others. And in the others one finds an impersonal spirit, one could say, no?

Rimbaud criticizes the self *through the other,* but as I said, the other is another self, another I. We need to make a radical critique of the other and of the self, that is to say, a critique of subjectivity. In parts of Lévi-Strauss we find a total criticism of subjectivity; and this is the importance of a philosopher like Wittgenstein. In criticizing language, he criticized the self, the ego. He has shown that 'I' is only a grammatical fiction. That is very important in my opinion.

I think the notion of *the other* must certainly be re-introduced, the *Other* with a capital O, not the other as *an other.* The other disappears. It is a combinatory expression, a vanishing message, and in this sense Buddhism becomes very modern, very modern because it is a criticism of the notion of the self, and at the same time, faced with the notion of 'the other and the self,' opposes to it this notion of a *self that has vanished,* the self that is an operation of the Cosmos.

Rudolf: You once said that the English writer has a direct link with his language, and the Spanish writer with his. But what about the Americans, where the principal languages are English and Spanish, and to a lesser extent Portuguese. Does, say, a Mexican writer such as yourself have a different kind of link? And which is more important, the 'written' or the 'spoken'?

Paz: I think that English writers, like Spanish writers, in a natural way feel themselves to be the inheritors of their respective traditions and use their language as if they own it. But we in America (and this also applies to French Canada, French Africa etc.) feel ourselves in a certain way *possessed* by our languages, possessed by strange powers, and we must, to a certain extent, revolt against the language:

161

take Eliot, Pound, Stevens and Carlos Williams; or Vallejo
and Neruda; or Drummond Andrade, Harold de Campos
and Augusto de Campos in Portuguese; and poets of the
French language like Aimé Césaire. With Césaire, French has
a different sound! The words are *spoken, danced, made
flesh.* I find a sort of *carnality,* a corporeal dimension in
his poetry, difficult to find in the poets of France itself.
The European languages become more carnal in America
and Africa.

Spanish poetry is much closer to French than to English poetry in the sense that one finds (especially in Latin
American poetry) the great themes of revolt, that is to say
of transgression, on the one hand, and at the same time the
idea that the world is a writing the poet can read, can translate, and that every poem is a translation of the world, and
a wound against the world. However in Spanish poetry
there is a primacy of the spoken word over the written
word. And that leads to another difference between French
and English poetry. In French there is a primacy of the
concept of writing (écriture). It signifies above all a visual
and intellectual experience. Have you ever seen the word
'writing' in an English or American poem?

Certainly 'writing' is not the same as 'écriture.' Conversely, *speech* is very difficult to translate into French.
Habla in Spanish, which is *speech* is not *parole.* In 'écriture' the eye has priority, which evokes a *solitary* experience, the individual reader before a text. In 'speech' I find
sound, not the eye but the ear, the ear and the tongue.
Since in the word *speech* we find the one who speaks and
the one who writes, there is already a premonition of the
collective experience of poetry.

Rudolf: You mention the collective experience of poetry.
In London last year you participated in the reading of a
collective poem of which you were one of the co-authors.
The poem, the *Renga,* aroused great interest. Will you say
something about it?

Paz: In modern times the idea was first preached by Lautréamont but the practice of collective poetry is very ancient. There is the Japanese Renga and certain Chinese
poems of the T'ang period. Surrealists like Breton, Char

162

and Eluard all made *admirable* collective poems. We have tried to do the same. We were of course influenced by the forbears I have mentioned. At the same time there was the combinatory idea, the combination not of signs but, for the first time, of the producers of signs, poets. We also introduced into collective poetry the notions of calculation and chance. As usual, chance occurs in the domain of rules, that is to say, chance appears as a *deviation* from the rule. Translation also had an important part. There were four poets: Tomlinson, Sanguinetti, Roubaud, Paz and thus the poem is written in four languages: English, Italian, French and Spanish, but in, I believe, a single poetic tradition. The plurality of languages is new and experimental for the traditional collective poem, but it is not unknown in modern poetry: Eliot, Pound and certain Spanish language poets.

Rudolf: Earlier, you touched on the question of criticism. And, you have written a book on Lévi-Strauss. What are your views on Structuralism? What can it do in this domain of criticism and poetry?

Paz: I don't think that the great scientific theories (and maybe Structuralism is scientific) are important for the poet unless the theory can become the flesh of a poem. There are no structuralist poets. Obviously structuralism is important in linguistics, in anthropology, and to a certain extent in criticism, but in criticism it is faced with a problem. Structuralism seeks out the invariants, the constants of a society or language, but what is important in literature is not the constants, but the variants. I am not interested in, no one is interested in, the constants that make Shakespeare, Dante, Lope de Vega and Racine alike. What is interesting is what makes them unique; and in the totality of Shakespeare's work, what makes each play different from the others. I don't see how structuralism can take this diversity of poetry into account.

However, structuralism is important because the structuralist critic is a poet in that every time he tries to reduce a text to certain invariants, he produces a new text. Every good structuralist translation, such as those by Barthes, becomes an aesthetic creation. So I don't know if it is a science but it has produced some beautiful works.

163

Here one might remind oneself that the poem itself is a critical act, Mallarmé's *poème-critique*. The nets we fish for words with are made with words. The criticism of language is made with language. Modern poetry, typically and admirably Surrealist poetry, is also a criticism of language, of the world, of poetry. Poetry is the transgression of poetry. We are condemned to this total ambiguity. The *poème-critique* or *texte* is the poem that continually *comes apart* (se défait), like those of the magazine *Siècle à Mains* or Americans like John Ashbery.

Rudolf: Modern music, modern art and concrete poetry are important to you, aren't they? One might cite your book on Duchamp or your poem dedicated to John Cage.

Paz: Concrete poetry is as old as poetry itself, as old as painting. But in the modern tradition concrete poetry begins with Mallarmé's *Un Coup de Dés* ... and this is admitted by the imitators of contemporary experimentation in the field: de Campos and the others in Brazil. Concrete poetry is a criticism of language, like all modern poetry. Romanticism made the poem a discourse of feeling: modern poets criticize the discourse, and concrete is the most radical criticism.

Duchamp is different. Painting is very important for me in that it is a system of forms, colours, lines, which are signs, which try to evoke or produce a presence, or in the case of certain painters, an absence ... in space. In literature you don't find signs immobilized in space, but signs that vanish. The text you read is a text that vanishes. *Words* are made to be read and the moment they are read the following words appear, followed in turn by other words. It is an art that unfolds over time, made from the appearance and disappearance of signs. Painting is a world where signs remain before you.

Duchamp introduced the notion of the critical painting in the same way as Mallarmé introduced that of the critical poem. He made painting transparent; he *annulled* painting, as Mallarmé annulled language. *La Grande Verre* is not a painting, not a picture, it is a moment of a picture, a transparency. Across *La Grande Verre* we see the world, or we see perhaps the absence that is the world, the great grimace that is the world. Through the irony of *La Grande Verre* and the lyricism of Mallarmé's *Un Coup de Dés* . . . we see the disappearance of the world and the advent of chance.

Cage interests me not only as a musician but as a poet and writer and my poem dedicated to him is above all dedicated to two of his books: *Silence* and *A Year from Monday*. We find in Cage the important idea of *disappearance, vanishing:* an idea found in Dada and the Surrealists but now in a different way as the vanishing of the sign. Signs, that is to say, art, vanish in favour of gestures. This is very Oriental and Cage is much influenced by Oriental, Buddhist thought. At the same time it is a very American gesture, very much of our continent.

☆   ☆   ☆

Manuel Durán

TOWARDS THE OTHER SHORE: THE LATEST
STAGE IN THE POETRY OF OCTAVIO PAZ

In the final pages of Carlos Fuentes' novel *Terra Nostra,*
several mysterious events occur which leave most readers
baffled. A hermaphroditic character appears. It is twelve
noon in Paris, but clocks everywhere remain silent, refusing
to give the time. Everything is shrouded in a pale solar light,
in a white, supernatural light. I would like to suggest that
here, as in other earlier instances in Fuentes' work, the poetry and *oeuvre* of Octavio Paz are able to make clear to us the
meaning of these strange presences in Fuentes' novel. And
conversely, these final pages of *Terra Nostra* help us in defin-
ing the meaning of Paz's poetry.

In an esoteric and at times grotesque form, Fuentes'
novel in the end, offers us a series of symbols of transformation and transcendence. We approach the other side of reality, of history, of everyday life. Behind innumerable pages
dedicated to history, philosophy, theology and magic, we are
ready for the mortal leap, the definitive transformation: the
contraries make a pact—the two sexes fuse into a single hermaphroditic being, a complete and visible symbol of androg-
ynous life, and we prepare to abandon historical time, the
time of chaos and mortality.[1] And here Fuentes does nothing
but follow in the footsteps that have left in our literary history some of Paz's greatest poems. The overcoming and

---

[1] It seems unnecessary to point out that Fuentes' novel appeared in
1975, while Paz's poems in which communion and "time outside
time" are exalted, belong to periods immediately or considerably before the novel. On the other hand, it is possible to show that Fuentes,
like Paz, a writer of vast culture, has read the works of Mircea Eliade
and Carl Jung in which these themes repeatedly appear. See Eliade's
Mephistopheles and the Androgyne (New York, 1965) and Carolyn G.
Heilbrun's *Towards Androgyny* (London, 1973) concerning hermaphroditic symbolism. And on the many similarities between Paz's
poetic thinking and Jung's work, see the interesting article by Richard
J. Callan, "Some Parallels between Octavio Paz and Carl Jung," *His-
pania* (vol. 60, Dec. 1977), pp. 916–926.

abolition of time for example, is a theme that appears several times in Paz, especially in *Viento entero (Wind from Every Compass Point)*, whose recurring theme is "the present is perpetual" where temporality is transcended through the merging of male and female gods:

El presente es perpetuo
En el pico del mundo se acarician
Shiva y Parvati

       Cada caricia dura un siglo
Para el dios y para el hombre

          Un mismo tiempo[2]

. . .

    (The present is perpetual
At the top of the world
Shiva and Parvati caress

       Each caress lasts a century
For god and for humanity

        The same time)

. . .

The pale sun of Fuentes also finds its source in the fusion of colors, whose union—light, is one of the facets of Paz's complex poem, *Blanco*. Fuentes' novel and Paz's poems (which are prior to it and the probable source of its inspiration) start from disintegration and advance toward a unity. As Juan García Ponce has written:

It is not difficult to see that two principal parallel lines run through the poetry of Octavio Paz within which the poet carries out and at the same time constructs his creative work, making as firm as destiny, the word's ultimate meaning. One of these lines is knowledge of the Fall, caused by an absence of natural Grace in the life of humankind, resulting in a feeling of uprootedness and a separation from a world before which humanity feels strange as a consequence of having lost original innocence. The other, partly a result of the attitude with

---

[2] *Ladera este* (Mexico, third ed., 1975), p. 107.

which Paz confronts that consciousness of the Fall, is a
faith in the power of artistic creation, in the power of
poetry—to reconcile us with a world fundamentally outside us—by its ability to restructure and reorder the
world through the power of the word.[3]

Already in 1948, in "Himno entre ruinas" ("Hymn
Among the Ruins"), we catch a glimpse of a solution in which
words play a primordial role:

. . .

La inteligencia al fin encarna
se reconcilian las dos mitades enemigas
y la conciencia-espejo se licúa,
vuelve a ser fuente, manantial de fábulas:
Hombre, árbol de imágenes,
palabras que son flores que son frutos que son actos.

(. . .
Intelligence becomes incarnate at last,
the two enemy halves are reconciled
and the mirror of consciousness is liquified,
to become a fountain again, source of fables:
Humankind, tree of images
words which are flowers which are fruits which are deeds.)

We begin with a paradox expressed again and again by Octavio
Paz himself—the tradition of contemporary poetry is a tradition of rupture. Style and vision of the world change with the
rapidity of growing, negating the earlier styles, the previous
visions, not allowing them to continue in any way. The poet,
just like the chimera the ancients spoke of, on changing, remains the same; and it is in this changing that the poet's fidel-
ity lies, the poet's being is to become. In this way we can refer
to a second period in the poetry of Juan Ramón Jiménez, to
various stages in Neruda's poetry, to a "latest" style in the

---

[3] La poesía de Octavio Paz," in *Aproximaciones a Octavio Paz*, ed. by
Angel Flores (Mexico, 1974), pp. 19-20. In the same book also see
Julio Ortega's "Viento entero: el tiempo en un día," pp. 200-208.
And Rachel Phillips' *The Poetic Modes of Octavio Paz* (Oxford, 1972),
pp. 38-9, 112, 115, 129-31.

poetry of Antonio Machado,

Paz's poetic work is so rich and varied that in order for us to go deeply into it, it is essential to mark the boundaries of certain zones on this vast map. I propose a rather simple division in three parts. "Himno entre ruinas" will form the first period of the poetry collected in *Libertad bajo palabra (Liberty on Parole)*. This will be followed by a transitional period composed again of "Himno entre ruinas," and by *Salamandra* and *Piedra de sol (Sun Stone)*. Finally, the second period will include everything from 1962 on, especially *Viento entero* (1965), *Blanco* (1967), *Ladera este* (1969), *El mono gramático (The Monkey Grammarian,* partly a prose poem, 1974) and *Vuelta* (1976).

Paz himself seems to have foreseen the direction his poetic evolution was going to take in a youthful phrase he wrote: "The poet driven by desire abandons solitude for communion."[4] Communion through comprehension, reconciliation, love—is to see our existence revealed in another being and partly merged with it. The other reveals and defines us. A solitary heart, Machado said, is no heart.

The path traveled by Paz in these last years is so considerable that we might speak of a complete transformation. I see rather a process of intensification and above all, the fulfillment of a poetic program already latent and sometimes explicit, in his earlier work. The Poet, in abandoning solitude, arrives at communion with beings, things and the world. If the earlier themes of freedom, destiny, death and eroticism do not entirely disappear, they are nevertheless transformed, surrounded by a new attitude, a new sensibility.

The typography also becomes modified, spread out as in the experiment in *Blanco,* which might be the first adaptation of Chinese scrolls in modern western poetry and even approaches at times, concrete poetry whose typography sketches an image. For Paz, as for Mallarmé, the silences and empty spaces also speak, are also meanings. The use of alternating and complementary fragments in the same poem, already present in *Salamandra,* is systematically amplified in *Ladera este,* in which Oriental influences remain purged, transformed and synthesized through a contrasting opposition

---

[4] Ramón Xirau in *Tres poetas de la soledad* (Mexico, 1955), pp. 39–70.

between short poems with frequent irony, mysterious at times, bringing to mind Japanese poetry and the long poems, sensual and pantheistic, inspired by Hindu culture. Pantheism and irony then are the two principal ingredients of this latter book, the two voices with which the Poet directs at his situation, the ebb and flow of the present.

This evolution and dialogue are carried out without Paz losing touch with his Western, Hispanic and Mexican roots. The memory and presence of the West intervene in a receptive form and integrate the Oriental experience. Paz's poetry stretches out to the universal in this second period because of it, not as an abstraction, but as a creative synthesis. Finally, we find in *Blanco* the most advanced, most ambitious example, maybe even the most successful, of this poetry of communion and synthesis. It is not necessary to point out that the more ambitious Paz's poetic program becomes, the more difficult it is to read his poems. I believe *Blanco* is his most difficult book so far (I confess I had to read it four or five times before I could comprehend it).

A good example of a short poem is "Aparición" (Apparition) in *Ladera este:*

> Si el hombre es polvo
> Esos que andan por el llano
> Son hombres
>
> (If humankind is dust
> Those who walk through the plains
> Are human)

It would be difficult to say more with fewer words. This brief, concentrated form reminds us, on the one hand, of Japanese haiku and of a syllogism, on the other. The beginning words "humankind is dust" are reminiscent of a Western Christian, medieval, ascetic tradition lasting until the Golden Age. But this abstract definition is modified immediately by the double impact of the title "Apparition" and the two final lines. We are suddenly reminded that the Poet writes from India, perhaps opposite a burning, dusty plain and those apparitions, those tiny, remote shapes covered by dust are our counterparts. Dust as a symbol of death remains transformed—until

170

what point depends on the reader, and in it resides in part, the riches of the poem; not in vain has Paz written that there exist as many poets as readers—in real dust, dust of a desolate plain. (We avoid, let it be said in passing, exaggerating the Oriental traces in this latest period of Octavio Paz. Already in his first period he was writing excellent "lapidary" or "Japanese inspired" poems such as are found in *Libertad bajo palabra:*

> Roe el reloj
> mi corazón
> buitre no, sino ratón.[5]

> [The clock gnaws at
> my heart
> not a vulture, but a rat.]

The evolution is then rupture but also continuation.)

The contrast between the short poems with their load of mystery or irony, and the long ones, with their vision of a cosmos in a rough swirling of activities that influence and interpenetrate, is probably what constitutes the internal organization of Paz's latest books, especially *Ladera este.* If we may compare a short poem to a photograph of the outer world, a photograph deformed and transmuted by the mind, experience, irony or the philosophical spirit of the Poet, then a large poem would have to be like the projection of a color film onto a screen of vast dimensions, in the course of which the mind and sensibility of the Poet speak with things and each time expand in order to embrace more aspects of an external world which is at the same time shaped and modified by the Poet's ego, until the bounds between inside and outside, you and I, above and below, begin to fade.

In these poems of Octavio Paz, the three roads to revelation, according to Ramón Xirau, are image, love and a sense of the sacred. Very close to Machado and Heidegger, Octavio Paz sees the poem as a being shaped by phrases whose intimate makeup is time. But if the poem is temporal, how does one specify its significance clearly?

Like Heidegger, for whom the essence of poetry may be

---

[5] Mexico, second ed., 1968, p. 45.

given from a few of Hölderlin's verses, Paz chooses a particular image formed by two phrases: "heavy as a stone," "light as a feather." What is the poetic image? Undoubtedly, the union of contraries. "The poet," Paz has said, "names things: these are feathers, those are stones. And suddenly affirms—the stones are feathers, this is that. The elements of the image do not lose their concrete and singular character. The stones continue being stones, rough, hard, impenetrable, sunny yellow or mossy green—heavy stones. And the feathers, feathers; light. The image turns out to be shocking because it defies the law of non-contradiction. To declare the contrary entity assaults the foundation of our thinking."[6] And Ramón Xirau observes:

> In other words, the image for Paz is essentially paradoxical and reveals simultaneously the unity and the vexing paradox which we are. The image discloses the contrary of logical thought that has dominated the West since Parmenides. It reveals our sameness and our otherness. It ends up by demonstrating that we are at the same time, ourselves and another. For Paz, the poetic experience resembles the experiences of the Orient—for which the horror of the "other" doesn't exist—and the expression of a few mystics of the West.[7]

Paz himself, in his "Carta a León Felipe" (Letter to León Felipe), points out some characteristics of his poetics:

> . . .
>
> Como los saltimbanquis
>
>   Andan por el aire
>
> Dos loros en pleno vuelo
>
>   Desafían al movimiento
>
> Y al lenguaje
>
>   ¡Míralos
>
>   Ya se fueron!
>
> Irradiación de unas cuantas palabras
>
> Es un aleteo

---

[6] *El arco y la lira* (Mexico, second ed., 1967), p. 99.
[7] *Octavio Paz: el sentido de la palabra* (Mexico, 1970), pp. 35 f.

El mundo se aclara
Sólo para volverse invisible

Aprender a ver oír decir
                    Lo instantáneo
Es nuestro oficio
                    ¿*Fijar vértigos?*
Las palabras
              Como los pericos en celo
Se volatilizan
              Su movimiento
Es un regreso a la inmovilidad

. . .

La poesía
              Es la ruptura instantánea
Instantáneamente cicatrizada
                         Abierta de nuevo
Por la mirada de los otros
                         La ruptura
Es la continuidad
. . .

                    (Ladera este, pp. 90–92)

(. . .
Like acrobats
              Flying through air
Two parrots in full flight
                    Defy motion
And language
              Look at them
                         Already gone!
Irradiation of a few words
Is a flapping of wings
                    The world making itself clear
Only to become invisible again

173

To learn to see to hear to say
                              The instantaneous
Is our trade
                    To get hold of vertigos?
Words
          Like these parakeets in heat
Dissipate themselves
                              Their movement
Is a return to immobility

. . .

Poetry
          is instantaneous rupture
Instantly healed
                    Cut open again
Through the meeting of another's eyes
                                        Rupture
Is continuity
. . .)

Poetry is then, a form of approaching close to "the other shore" "there where contraries make a pact," a way of transcending solitude and the poverty of the ego locked up in itself. Which leads us to observe that the Orient for Paz, expressed as a lived and cultural experience in which his poetry has reached its prime, has a tendency radically opposed and contrary to the Oriental experience of Pablo Neruda. The Orient absorbed Neruda, locking him up in the treasures of his subconscious. Paz is opened up by the Orient, fusing his experience and personality with a vaster and vaster present and horizon. At the end of "Vrindaban," Paz writes:

. . .

Tengo hambre de vida y también de morir
Sé lo que creo y lo escribo
Advenimiento del instante
                              El acto
El movimiento en que se esculpe
Y se deshace el ser entero

174

Conciencia y manos para asir el tiempo
Soy una historia
                    Una memoria que se inventa
Nunca estoy solo
Hablo siempre contigo Hablas siempre conmigo
A oscuras voy y planto signos

                              (Ladera este, pp. 62–63)

(. . .
I am hungry for life and for death too
I know what I believe and I write it
Coming of the instant
                    The act
The movement in which whole being
Is sculpted and destroyed
Consciousness and hands to seize time
I am a history
                    A memory that invents itself
I am never alone
I always talk with you You always with me
In the dark I go and plant signs)

Contrast Paz's "I am never alone" with Neruda's phrase in
Residencia en la tierra, a book directly influenced by his Eastern experience: "Estoy solo entre materias desvencijadas" (I
am alone among broken down substances).

Viento entero, one of Paz's longest, most important and
characteristic poems of this "Eastern period," is a good example of the technique with which the Poet articulates and
by saying it in this way "ennobles" a series of experiences
appearing at first sight, disordered and chaotic. The *link* in
the end concludes by means of a repetition of a central theme
—"El presente es perpetuo" (The present is perpetual). Each
incident is like a brief notation in a travel diary:

          . . .
En los claros de silencio
                    Estallan
Los gritos de los niños
                    Príncipes en harapos

A la orilla del río atormentado
Rezan orinan meditan
                    El presente es perpetuo
Se abren las compuertas del año
                              El día salta
          Agata
. . .

(. . .
In the clear silences
                    Explode
The children's cries
                    Princes in rags
On the shore of the tormented river
They pray they piss they plan
                              The present is perpetual
The floodgates of the year are opened
                              The day bursts
          Agate
. . .)

The dignification of the material is carried out through images
and mythology (I believe this is one of the modern poems
Góngora would have understood immediately). The beloved
woman is described briefly: ". . . Si el fuego es agua / Eres
una gota diáfana . . ." (. . . If fire is water / You are a limpid
drop . . .). The mountains are: ". . . Soles destazados / Petrificada tempestad ocre . . ." (. . . Carved out suns / Petrified
ochre storms . . .).

El puño de la sangre golpea
                    Puertas de piedra
. . .

(The fists of blood pounded
                    Doors of rock
. . .)

La noche entra con todos sus árboles
Noche de insectos eléctricos y fieras de seda
. . .

176

(The night comes in with all its trees
Night of electric insects and beasts of silk
. . .)

And we enter in this way into a zone of vertigos and mystery
in which everything is possible beneath the remote gaze of
the gods:

. . .
    Los universos se desgranan
Un mundo cae
      Se enciende una semilla
Cada palabra palpita
       Oigo tu latir en la sombra
Enigma en forma de reloj de arena
        Mujer dormida

. . .
Emigran los espacios
     El presente es perpetuo
En el pico del mundo se acarician
Shiva y Parvati
    Cada caricia dura un siglo
Para el dios y para el hombre
      Un mismo tiempo
Un mismo despeñarse

. . .
Yo veo a través de mis actos irreales
El mismo día que comienza
     Gira el espacio
Arranca sus raíces el mundo
No pesan más que el alba nuestros cuerpos
      Tendidos

(. . .
  The universes separate
A world crashes down
    A seed is ignited
Each word throbs
    I hear your pulse in the shade

Riddle shaped hourglass

        Sleeping woman

. . .

Spaces migrate

        The present is perpetual

At the top of the world

Shiva and Parvati caress

        Each caress lasts a century

For god and for humanity

        The same time

To hurl yourself down

. . .

I see through my unreal acts

The same day that begins

        Goes around spaces

The world tears up its roots

Our stretched out bodies weigh no more

        Than the dawn)

Flow and return of consciousness and the external world, point and counterpoint and the eternal, the latter reinforced by the words "always" and "perpetual" that appear repeatedly, Paz's poem is made up of contrary elements coordinated in a unity, a synthesis that leaves undestroyed each concrete experience except order and meaning. The eternal and fleeting come to an agreement and coexist. The erotic and sacred experiences strike us very closely, since, as Paz has written:

> . . . These are acts that spring forth from the same fountain. At different levels of existence we leap wanting to reach the other shore. Communion, to mention a familiar example, brings about a change in the nature of the believer. The sacred food transmutes us. And that being "others" is nothing but a recapturing of our original nature or condition. "Woman," Novalis said, "is the highest bodily food." . . . The idea of the return—present in every religious act, in every myth and even in utopias—is the force of the gravity of love. Woman exalts us, makes us get out of ourselves and simultaneously makes us return. To fall: to be again.[8]

---

[8] *El arco y la lira*, p. 135.

And finally we reach *Blanco*, perhaps Paz's most difficult poem. If *Viento entero* expressed a precarious yet spar-
kling plenitude, a cosmic confidence, *Blanco* might seem to us
at the beginning a cautious and solipsistic poem, a poem of
words and about the word, the word that looks at itself in the
mirror, the word that bites its tail and withdraws into itself.
On this poem are cast the shadows of Mallarmé, Georges Bataille, and maybe even Zen Buddhism with its instinctive mistrust before intellectual constructions of language.

If we could see the world through words, if only with
words we could get hold of and seize the chaos that surrounds
us, what then would the very foundation of the word be?
Let us reread another fragment from "Carta a León Felipe"
that might well serve as a prologue for *Blanco:*

   . . .
Las palabras
         Como los pericos en celo
Se volatilizan
          Su movimiento
Es un regreso a la inmovilidad

No nos queda dijo Bataille
Sino escribir comentarios
            Insensatos
Sobre la ausencia de sentido del escribir
Comentarios que se borran
             La escritura poética
Es borrar lo escrito
        Escribir
Sobre lo escrito
       Lo no escrito
Representar la *comedia* sin desenlace
Je ne puis parler d'une absence de sens
Sinon lui donnant un sens qu'elle n'a pas

La escritura poética es
          Aprender a leer
El hueco de la escritura
         En la escritura

(*Ladera este*, p. 91)

(. . .
Words
  Like these parakeets in heat
Dissipate themselves
    Their movement
Is a return to immobility

Nothing remains for us said Bataille
But to write foolish
    Commentaries
On the absence of meaning in writing
Commentaries that erase themselves
      To write poetry
Is to erase the written
    To write
On the written
    The unwritten
To perform the *comedy* without an ending
Je ne puis parler d'une absence de sens
Sinon lui donnant un sens qu'elle n'a pas

To write poetry is
    Learning to read
The empty space of writing
      In the writing
. . .)

 Blanco is a poem that, like the novel *Rayuela* by Julio Cortázar, can be read in many ways. The large central poem (about 80% of the text) is a long discourse on the word and silence, on the foundation of the word. To the right and left rise, like short walls, like flanked towers, two other poems—a love poem and a poem dedicated to the sensations. As if with the presence of love and the sensations Paz should want to give life and sensualize what in some other way would result in an exceedingly intellectual and dry exercise. The word leans on itself, it questions itself about its own being. We see

born, slowly, with effort, the words "sunflower," "river."
But Paz's flower is much more concrete than Mallarmé's
l'absente de tout bouquet:

> . . .
>
> Alto en su vara
> (Cabeza es una pica),
> Un girasol
>
> . . .
>
> Flor
> Ni vista ni pensada:
> Oída,
>
> Aparece
> Amarillo
> Cáliz de consonantes y vocales
> Incendiadas.
> . . .
>
> (. . .
> High on its shaft
> [Head on a pike]
> A sunflower
>
> . . .
>
> Neither seen nor thought:
> Heard
>
> Appears
> Yellow
> Chalice of consonants and vowels
> Burning.)

The Poet advances by means of paradox:

> . . .
>
> La irrealidad de lo mirado
> Da realidad a la mirada
>
> . . .
>
> (. . .
> The unreality of the seen

Makes real the seeing
        . . .)

One must know how to say No and Yes at the same time. We
got out of trouble not by using the traditional linear logic,
but thanks to an ambiguous, circular one:

        . . .
        El espíritu
        Es una invención del cuerpo
        El cuerpo
        Es una invención del mundo
        El mundo
        Es una invención del espíritu
        . . .

        (. . .
        The spirit
        Is an invention of the body
        The body
        An invention of the world
        The world
        An invention of the spirit
        . . .)

And the philosophical poem is contaminated at last by eroticism before a young woman ". . . desnuda / Como una sílaba
. . ." (. . . naked / As a syllable . . .) whose body ". . . Visto /
Desvanecido / Da realidad a la mirada" (. . . Seen / Vanished /
Makes real the seeing). And the mirror breaks: the image lives.
Through the presence of another human being, a presence
seized and aroused by the word and its meanings, language remains well-founded, established, in this poem. And in it, as in
all Paz's poetry, contraries make a pact and are reconciled and
in so doing reach the plenitude of their own being.

trans. from the Spanish by Kosrof Chantikian

☆   ☆   ☆

Margaret Sayers Peden

A "MEDITATION" ON *BLANCO*

Since 1973, when I offered a graduate seminar on Octavio Paz and Carlos Fuentes and included *Blanco* in the readings, I have been fascinated by the poem, one of the most important, I believe, in Paz's canon. This special Paz edition of *KOSMOS* offers me an opportunity to say a few things about the poem, about its structure and about how it transcends the limitations of the printed page. I also want to explain why *Blanco* is a mandala.

The reader's immediate impression of the poem, one that necessarily precedes the perception of its content, is one of form and structure. This is a conscious effect, carefully orchestrated, and through innovative typography strives to liberate poetry from the flat, one-dimensional pages of the traditional book.

My students were so struck by this aspect of *Blanco,* they suggested the poem be suspended from the ceiling of a gallery, and in that way the words could truly be liberated. As the poem is largely about word and language, their interest in that liberation seemed not unrelated.

One does not turn the pages of this book; the pages or leaves unfold into one long, accordion-pleated strip of paper. The words flow from the book, escaping the confines of the covers. The result is not linear, however, but rather, circular. The last leaf can be joined to the first to create a circular, or eternal, book. Typography is an integral part of the whole. The typeface changes frequently, as form reinforces and at times creates content; and the two colors of the typeface of the sections of double columns further emphasize the visual impact of this poetic construct. The white spaces (the *blancos)* are equally significant. We remember Paz's essays on John Cage, and hear the cadences of silence in this poem. In one way, *Blanco* may be read as music. The sections are movements. The last movement recapitulates the themes of the earlier movements. The point/counterpoint of the dual passages is immediately evident.

The jacket copy of *Blanco* errs in one essential point. It

defines its form as spiral. This is a mistake. The circle is Paz's form. And *Blanco* is a circle. But it is also a square. It is a mandala, the circle squared, the square made a circle.

The central poem, centered typographically and thematically, follows the progression of the word from silence to silence. The poems set in double columns, sometimes independent, sometimes fused, are, in the left-hand column, four love poems, and, in the right-hand column, four poems involving various degrees of sensation. These basic ground rules are clearly outlined in the notes to the reader and remind me of Cortázar's instructions to the reader in *Rayuela,* also an attempt to transcend traditional form. Eighteen of the twenty-three leaves of *Blanco* are devoted to the central theme. The first and last six leaves are of similar typeface; the remaining, intervening leaves of the central poem are of a different face. Hence the typeface suggests that the poem is circular and that the last leaf is connected with the first.

In the beginning, there is silence, a latent seed *(sin nombre, sin habla,* lf 1). Though language is empty *(deshabitado,* lf 2), we sense a pulse *(late una lámpara,* lf 2). A sunflower sheds "burned" light in the shadow, but a truly yellow flower appears, a chalice of "blazing consonants and vowels" (lf 3). With an admonition borrowed from Livingstone (Patience, patience, lf 5), the witness to the birth throes of language is aware of a pulsing, a presentiment (lf 5). Then on leaf six the progression of the word is momentarily interrupted for the identification and localization of a human presence, one we have noted previously *(una mano,* lf 3; *mi frente,* lf 5), and which builds on this leaf to an insistent *I am* (lf 6). Following this hiatus, the focus returns to language, which is described as expiation (lf 6) and propitiation (lf 6). The inadequacy, the inefficacy, of the word is made dismally apparent. It is "polishing bones" and "refining silences to transparency" (lf 7). Language is symbolized as "calcined earth," as "barbs and thorns in eyes" (lf 9). Three buzzards perch on a wall (lf 9). The sun is unjust (lf 10). Even so, this is the climactic moment. Movement erupts from sterility *(Tambores, tambores, tambores,* lf 10). Though the blackness of the buzzards is continued in the blackness of crows, the human-who-is-creator *(te golpeo cielo / Tierra te golpeo,* lvs 10–11) smites the earth and water rushes forth. The earth's belly trembles, her seeds burst open, the word is born (lf 11).

In this progression one notes a rising and falling rhythm: imminence (lf 2) is followed by non-existence (lf 3). A stirring (lf 5) is stilled by sterility (lf 7). Finally, light and sound accompany the "greening" of birth. Parallel to the ebb and flow of the birth process of the word is the subtler, but complementary, emergence of human presences that reach their nadir *(a todas nos aplasta,* lf 10) immediately before the smiting of the earth that temporarily frees both humanity and word.

The instant of harmony (we know this *instante resplandeciente* from other Paz poems) cannot last. *Now* becomes *past.* The ensuing *now* announces a new movement, a pilgrimage towards transparency. The senses reel as the world becomes more rarefied (lf 13). Abstracted, speech becomes sign, and words lose their substance. In the subsequent progression towards "the empty face of oblivion" (lf 14), the former creator finds himself in a void *(Pierdo mi sombra, / Avanzo / Entre bosques impalpables,* lvs 14–15). Reality, even suprareality, dissolves *([el] espacio que se desvanece / En pensamientos que no pienso,* lf 15).

At this point, on leaf 18, the type, a formal component of major contextual importance, changes to the face related to the face of the first leaf of the poem. Language again becomes fragmented, and the arrangement of the words on the page is suggestive of a return (either a turning back or a movement forward) to the first leaf. This interruption is strategic, as are the opening words of the leaf: *En el centro.* The tempo of the oppositions—that is, the seeming dichotomies so essential to Paz's poetry in general, and to *Blanco* specifically—is increased. *Sí* and *no* are used as a kind of repeated litany, and often can be attached either to the words that precede them or those that follow. The emptiness, the inadequacy and inefficacy, of the word is reiterated *(aire son,* lf 18), *Inacabada, Inacabable* (lvs. 18–19), but with reiteration a new element is introduced that creates the fusion we have come to expect from Paz's oppositions: the lover *(Tus pasos en el cuarto vecino,* lf 19). Now the threads of the poems set in double columns, the poems on love and sensation, fuse with and blend into the central poem about language. "Two enamored syllables," *no y sí,* fall between the breasts of the beloved. A paradox is posed, or a tautology: "If the world is real, the word is unreal. If the word is real, the world is fissure, splendor, vortex" (lf 20). Yes. No. Real. Unreal. Then the inevitable and eternal circularity of Paz's cosmology is spelled out:

> The spirit / is an invention of the body
> The body / is an invention of the world
> The world / is the invention of the spirit
>
> (lf 22).

And the silence is resolved. Reality *(El mundo)* resides in the lover's spirit *(Haz de tus imágenes)* and the lover's body *(Tu cuerpo / Derramado en mi cuerpo). This* silence is not empty, but inhabited. Inevitably, however, the resolution will dissolve and the cycle will begin again, returning to *el comienzo* of the first leaf.

Several very pleasing things are happening in this progression from empty silence to inhabited silence. Among them, we note the cohesiveness of the use of the symbols of fire (lf 3), earth (lf 9), water (lf 11), and air (lf 13), which are symbols of the "four moments" of Paz's love poems and contrapuntally-echoed poems on sensation. Further cohesive strength is found in the recapitulatory lines of the last two leaves, on which all the important components of the poem are gathered together. Unity, oneness, is stressed as Paz repeats the lines that synthesize the four sets of contrapuntal poems—*La pasión de la brasa compasiva* (lf 4), *La transparencia es todo lo que queda* (lf 8), *El mundo haz de tus imágenes* (lf 12), and *La irrealidad de lo mirado / Da realidad a la mirada* (lf 17)—which, in turn, renew the role of the four elements. And to underline the presence of the lover in the last movement of the poem, Paz repeats the line that marks the lover's appearance, *Tus pasos en el cuarto vecino* (lf 19), and the line that emphasizes the lover's continuing presence, *tu cuerpo / . . . derramada en mi cuerpo*, from the love poem on lf 16.

But to return to a key phrase in the poem, *En el centro* (lf 18): the significance of this makes it impossible to read the poem as a simple ascending and descending arc between identical silences. Rather, leaves 1 to 10 are ascent, leaf 11 is the apex of one arc *(Verdea la palabra),* and leaves 11 to 17 are descent. On leaf 18, the type and the rhythm change. On 19, the lover enters. Leaves 20, 21, and 22 pose paradoxes and the field of all possibilities. Leaves 22 and 23 offer the resolution and at the same time suggest a return to the beginning. The silence that precedes *En el centro* is uninhabited. The lover shares the silence that follows.

Blanco is a figure composed of many rhythms and many frequencies operating on many planes: a point I made at the beginning, that the poem is freed from the limitations of the printed page. If you have seen the plastic, multidimensional sets of tic-tac-toe, you will recognize the following analogy. Just as a simple game played on a one-dimensional surface is lifted to challenging complexity in space, *Blanco* transcends the printed page to assume a greater complexity in space and time.

In a related matter, a small illustration may serve to demonstrate one of the many ways Paz frees his poem from time. He assigns a descriptive quality to a word, then with a minute change, projects that quality into the infinite. In the opening lines, word, or language is "unheard." A shift in syllables and that specific quality is launched into unboundness: the "unheard" word becomes "unhearable" (inaudible). On leaf 19, the same technique is applied to the page on which the word appears. It is first *Inacabada,* an incomplete or unfinished page, but the intensity of the description is augmented by a simple change of final syllables: the page becomes "uncompletable"*(Inacabable).* Paz also shifts his words from their traditional space by self-consciously commenting on them within the context of the work. "The sky blackens / like this page," he comments on leaf 10. Words, on leaf 18, are like "this insect / fluttering between the lines / of the page." Similarly, ". . . thought / fluttering / among the words" (lf 19). This technique is becoming a commonplace in contemporary Latin American novels, which one critic has said can be read only as satiric essays on the novel, but it is not, to my knowledge, widely used in poetry.

In my discussion of the rhythms of the central poem in *Blanco,* I have been using a number of terms which are not my own. When I was a graduate student, a fellow student, Raymond Souza, wrote an article on Paz which is so quintessential in its definition of Paz's ontological perceptions that I

187

have ever since wondered why it hadn't been written before and how we can escape rewriting it every time a comment is ventured on Paz's poems. I knew Edmond Wilson's shock of recognition when I read that article. Souza's point is that Paz's poetry is ruled by a pattern of dualism that consistently resolves into unity. Souza's formula is Hegelian, posing thesis/antithesis resolved into synthesis as the basic figure in Paz's poetry. He might have said that Paz's perceptions are more Eastern than Western, fusing seeming contradictions into the all-encompassing One. He might have used other formulas. But the frame for truth is not as important as the fact that his point is irrefutable: oppositions that blend into harmony are a basic rhythm in Paz's poems.

Blanco is permeated with this rhythm. First, in the broadest sense, the opposition of the poem of the central columns *(el comienzo . . . la palabra en la punta de la lengua,* lf 1) and the poems of the double columns about woman *(Muchacha / tú ríes)* and the senses *(los sentidos se abren,* lf 4) is resolved and fused together in the final leaves when word and woman become one sensual figure. Within this larger rhythm are smaller rhythms, for example, the thesis/antithesis of the dual sections printed in red and black. These two tensions are resolved into a synthesis that is visual typographically, as well as perceivable in the context. Each of these four interludes ends with a single line (the last, with two) that is centered between the two columns, combining the two entities and resolving them in the figure of the element that is the symbol of that section:

> *La pasión de la brasa compasiva*   (fire, lf 4)
> *La transparencia es todo lo que queda*   (water, lf 8)
> *El mundo haz de tus imágenes*   (earth, lf 12)
> *La irrealidad de lo mirado / Da realidad a la mirada*
> (air, lf 17).

And in the descending rhythm of oppositions, we find small units, individual pairs, of contrasting words. The first leaf offers clear examples:

grávida	*nula*
inocente	*promiscua*
cimiento	*simiente*

In addition, we see examples of visual contrast in which meanings are not opposed, but the visual arrangement provides the *effect* of contrast:

> *inaudita*   *inaudible*
> *sin nombre*   *sin habla*   (lf 1).

These visual oppositions are resolved in typographical harmony, while the oppositions of meaning are resolved in the fusion of the final two leaves.

While we speak of a descending order of rhythms, from the broad to the narrow, we must remember that within this order, though each rhythmic frequency has its individual vibration, the final resolution is one of harmony—from many to *one*.

But why does *Blanco* suggest a mandala? This is not the first of Paz's poems to approach the form. One thinks of the circular structure of *Piedra de sol,* and remembers that the sun stone *itself* is a mandala. And the concrete poems of *Discos* are very much like the mandala, turning around a central pin and revealed through pie-shaped cut-outs in the top disk.

The *New Columbia Encyclopedia* defines a mandala as "a concentric diagram, having spiritual or occult significance, in the form of a square, a circle, or combination, usually quartered." I find this to be an excellent description of *Blanco.* *Blanco* is an insistently *geometric* work, the square and the circle assault the reader's sensibilities, and it is the mandala that readily accommodates these irreconcilable forms. *Blanco*'s squareness or "quarteredness," obviously suggested itself to the jacket designer. On both case and book the square appears in mirrored images. Further quartered, the central poem is interrupted and surrounded by the four movements of the love and sensation poems, which are interjected every fourth leaf (lvs 4, 8, 12, and 16). This suggests the four corners surrounding the center in the mandala, and the poem about the word is the center of *Blanco.* The mandala often represents the four seasons, or the four basic elements, and in *Blanco* the four elements of water, fire, earth, and air, are a consistently unifying force. Four colors represent the differing stages of the word (yellow, red, green, and blue). Finally, squareness is suggested in the visual layout of the two-columned poems.

But the square of *Blanco* is circled. The typeface suggests that the end leads to the beginning. The "center" of the poem is "the word." The words *En el centro* are like a watershed: they define the difference between the silence that exists without woman and the silence that is inhabited, thanks to the spirit and body of woman. The generative circle of spirit> body>world>spirit is imperative in the poem. A mandala is a visual harmony of seemingly contradictory figures. In a mandala all polarities are resolved in the center. I see such harmony and resolution in *Blanco.*

In many parts of the world a mandala is a visual vehicle for profound meditation. *Blanco* is such a vehicle. It offers a meditation on the essential themes in Paz's poetry—woman, world, and word—essential entities. If we approach *Blanco* as a mandala, we may in our meditation enjoy, even if only for an *instante resplandeciente,* Paz's gift of harmony and oneness.*

☆   ☆   ☆

---

*I found out recently what I should have known before: *Paz* referred to a mandala in his explanatory notes in *Ladera este.* I was chagrined I hadn't been aware of this before I made my own naive "discovery," but in the long run, I have been pleased. Paz intended the reader to see a mandala, I saw a mandala.

Ricardo Gullón

REVERBERATION OF THE STONE

In an anthology of modern poetry limited to the ten
best poems of the twentieth century, two written in Spanish
would rightfully take a place. Next to Rilke and Pessoa, not
far from Eliot and Ungaretti, near Yeats and Pasternak, close
to Seferis and Valéry, I (anthologizing is always a personal
matter) would include works of Juan Ramón Jiménez and
Octavio Paz. (If it were a matter of books rather than poems,
neither Jorge Guillén's *Cántico* nor César Vallejo's *Trilce*
could be kept from this list). And the poems which in my
judgment would best represent Jiménez and Paz (though I
believe he would not agree) are "Espacio" (Space) and *Piedra
de sol (Sun Stone)*. In the first instance the selection seems
indisputable; in the second, perhaps there is room to show
Blanco can vie with *Piedra de sol* in its modernity. Yet it is
precisely the assimilation and interpretation of the modern
in the eternal which makes me prefer the latter.

Piedra de sol has been widely discussed and commented
on; but occasionally someone like José Emilio Pacheco, who
like Paz, being both a poet and a Mexican, gives an account
of things most other critics have neglected. Pacheco, in his
essay, "Description of *Piedra de sol,"* begins by noting the
noble quality of the poem—which is no exaggeration since it
is a masterpiece. I've used the adjective "eternal"; this is a
word not to be used carelessly. Open poetry and closed poetry;
line and circle; limpid and hermetic. A space as immense as
Blake's "grain of sand," with horizon and time before and
after the word. Having placed *Piedra de sol* under the invoca-
tion of Artemis and, more precisely, under the enigma created
by Gérard de Nerval in his sonnet "Artémis" (his four lines
serve as an epigraph to Paz's verses), the poem shows clearly
it is intentionally and necessarily mysterious. Mysterious, but
as I said, also limpid. Images that suggest the one and its contrary, verticality and horizontality; for example: "sauce de
cristal" (willow of crystal), "chopo de agua" (poplar of water),
"surtidor que el viento arquea" (gushing fountain curved by
the wind), "árbol . . . danzante" (tree . . . dancing), opening
up to a poetic space in which all evocations and transformations

191

will be possible.

They will be possible thanks to the poetic activity of an imagination whose shape expresses symbolically that which, by taking root so deeply, cannot be verbalized in any other way. Symbolization: reversion toward the outside of interiorized intuitions, certainly, but actually caused by exterior impulses. Paz writes with a passion scarcely masked by the beauty of the writing which proves that intuition, although it comes from shadow, is genuinely illuminating, and conversely obscures and clouds the translucent: "voy por las transparencias como un ciego" (I go through transparencies like a blindman). It could not be any other way since the universe through which the Poet passes is a body: "piernas de luz, vientre de luz" (legs of light, belly of light); woman is his city: his womb, "plaza soleada" (sunny plaza); her breasts, "iglesias donde oficia la sangre" (churches where blood is celebrated). The inversion of the images serves an identifying function: the world is an organism and the female body a world: "ciudad" (city), "muralla" (wall), "paraje de sal, rocas y pájaros" (place of salt, rocks and birds). World and woman are labyrinths as well as inventions of the voice which speaks them, of the vision that courses through them and dreams them. Thus the expression has cosmic force and desire, and the innocence and ferocity of an animal: "los tigres beben sueño en esos ojos" (tigers drink sleep in those eyes), a desire made gentle as it touches this body in thoughts. Rarely has love been expressed with such total consciousness. And even if there were no other evidence, these six or seven verses which I am reading would be enough to place Octavio Paz among the finest erotic poets of our time—where sadly, the female body has been degraded into a thing.

Woman in this beautiful constellation is energetic and energizer. If by desiring woman men fertilize and transform her, they are at the same time fertilized by her "boca de agua" (mouth of water), by contact with the nature and spirit which she embodies. Expanding these quotations would simply show the extent to which Paz's verses are impregnated and determined by a metaphorical chain in which image on image illuminates a conception of woman as universe.

The poem revolves while the poet roams through the galleries that Antonio Machado scoured in dreams. Paz's are "corredores sin fin de la memoria" (corridors of endless memory), memories that are forgotten and arrive from very far to install themselves in the image of the poem, in the images which are the poem. To search for the form of these forgotten memories intending to recover them without their being altered seems a desperate attempt; but it is not since the text summons a continuity of evocations that creates and re-creates them. We read: "busco sin encontrar" (I search without finding). Such a declaration is inexact; through writing Paz has discovered the space and time through which the poem flows and in it his own image and likeness: weighed down by mystery, feeling his way, falling, accidentally slipping—all truly marvelous since to stumble is to hit against something—the revealing word, the flash of vision, symbol that defines exactly the imprecise, which gives shape to the ineffable.

Characters added to the text first as images, now appear with a face and name: Melusina, Laura, Isabel, Persephone, Mary, . . . allusions within the text that expand prodigiously the space within the poem; prodigious because how otherwise explain legend, myth, history, suddenly turning up to add complexity to the cipher of the text. We now are made to recall the potentiality of woman as magic: Melusina as fairy and serpent; Persephone as clear youthfulness and springtime (Kora) and queen of Hades; Mary—carpenter's wife and queen of the heavens. Myths, legends—and poetry; poetry of love incarnated in Laura de Noves (who loved Petrarch) and Isabel Freyre (who loved Garcilaso). Archetypes of absolute authenticity, characters of a metamorphosis provoked by the variation of myth. For Paz, this woman has "todos los rostros y ninguno" (all faces and none). It is Woman, Eternal Female, and immortalized in this way it is not strange that the Poet should turn to forms of expression tinged with religiosity. Pacheco has pointed out that the invocations found in this passage form a litany like Catholics appealing to the Virgin to intercede for us before God. "In *Piedra de sol,*" he observes, "the *I* addresses a remark to the beloved one, mediator between humanity and nature in the language of divine affection just as mystics have elevated their prayers to God in the language of concerned humans." This attitude and method of composition are suggestive of San Juan de la Cruz, Fray Luis de León and even of that passionate and wise king who wrote the "Song of Songs." And here one gives up a temptation much explored by criticism: that of singing the human to the divine, exalting passion to the dignity of God's love. It is clear, as well, that the litany of the lyrical voice does not reverberate in one direction alone: "reina de serpientes" (serpent queen), "fuente en la peña" (fountain in the rock), "pastora de los valles submarinos" (shepherd of underwater valleys), "guardiana del valle de los muertos" (guardian of the valley of the dead), correspond to mythical figures mystics never thought of.

The Poet conceives the poem as a struggle against time, a structure built with the most elusive material, the word, resistant to a vision, which acquires consistency and reality only through that word. Inventive word, instrument and substance from which verbal space is born, from which vision finds its privileged zone. The function of verse, Paz has said, "consists in reinventing time" and in reinventing it in order to transform the instant into the eternal. Poetry, Antonio Machado had warned, is "word in time." Never more so than in *Piedra de sol*, but with this addition: in the time and space of transfiguration. Slowly experience emerges in form; that is, form is the form of experience which goes on inventing itself in the poem. At this stage the poem "gives of itself," grows from itself and is as much energy as movement. Each line responds to the preceding one and postulates the next. A system in which the metonymical chain strengthens its links in unusual ways: name requires face, instant seeks centuries, dream asks for image, and from these requests correspondences emerge that emphasize reiteration in the variation:

> todos los nombres son un solo nombre,
> todos los rostros son un solo rostro,
> todos los siglos son un solo instante

> (all names are one name
> all faces a single face
> all centuries an instant)

The repetition in the first two lines suggest, even demand, an equivalence in the third. Perfection of the verse in which neither rhythm nor tone nor intuition vary. The connection is perfect as it was before in the presentation of the litany. Behind the reduction of diversity into harmony, the word we have waited for enters the poem: "death," antithesis and complement of love. Time resolves itself in death, destroys itself by the only act of being (". . . madura hacia dentro de sí mismo / y a sí mismo se bebe y se derrama") (. . . ripening inward / drinking and scattering itself) and in its mortality humankind recognizes and identifies itself with it. The most dramatic exclamation emerges now: "oh vida por vivir y ya vivida" (oh life to live and already have lived).

The voice that is saying and making the poem returns from present to future, burns the stages of time and feels itself already outside the abode of the instant, in a duration that is a pure going beyond, dust and smoke. Who guides the Poet in this descent to the depths of time? Woman from the beginning is not yet light but faithfully shadow, instrument of destruction. The lover has seen in Melusina the serpent which she reverts to periodically (tu atroz escama . . . brillar verdosa al alba") (your cruel scale . . . shining greenish at dawn) and has recognized in this fairy-tale monster the emblem of the human condition. Change of tone and vocabulary—in order to record the drama of the situation, the ambiguity of the times: the mother sees the father in the son; life is death and death "vida verdadera" (authentic life).

Can the voice which invents the poem identify itself? Is it one voice only? It knows neither its name nor who it is nor who that woman is nor the other who may walk at its side. But history saves it and gives it a past, a past of tangible reality touched by the fingers of memory. The name of this past is Carmen; it happened in Oaxaca or in Paris or more tense and unequivocal, in Madrid in 1937, amidst a war and on a square where there was then and is still a hotel for the Poet. All of this—facts, figures—is like the artist's signature in the corner of a painting, authenticating and identifying it.

Five lines are enough to introduce a situation, summarize a drama: the Spanish Civil war, the irruption of violence in calmness, the death of innocent ones. Death and love are joined; an exercise in continuity that brings together contraries and complements: bombs fall and bodies bind themselves together in copulation that will engender new life. And to whom does this spirit of passion speak? To woman, to its shadow, to itself? Mainly to itself, to its "others," emerging specters in the writing and at times determinants of its direction. What it says of love, of transfiguration in and through love, does not extend to reconstitute a personal experience but to discover in the potentiality of the word the greatness of this transformation of love. What a shock that this emotion is invented and made sacred this way ("todo se transfigura y es sagrado") (everything is transfigured and sacred) in this center of the world which is the bedroom!

I am opening myself up to a level of meaning that does not present major difficulties of interpretation, but it is advisable to warn the complexity of *Piedra de sol* is greater than has up to now been noted. Perhaps the visionary temptation should be emphasized and the peculiar texture of this vision, as in Lorca's *Poet in New York,* made up of threads of visible and invisible reality. Octavio Paz puts his hand into this clarity and contagion of his ardor, almost driven by its fever, raising it to the enigmatic to which I referred in the beginning.

Finally, Héloïse arrives. Paz was, I believe, waiting for her. (As he waited for her in Jiménez's "Espacio" where she appears and later Abélard, whose castrated condition is recalled by both Poets). Héloïse—absolute love and sex—sacrificed by an imbecile. This is the point where Paz, in speaking of love, oscillates between gentleness and burning passion and raises Abélard's curse to eloquence.

> mejor ser lapidado
> en las plazas que dar vuelta a la noria
>
> (better to be stoned to death
> in the town square than tread the mill).

Again and again myths. History makes and unmakes them; analogous in its expressiveness (in its meaning); different in its literalness. Assassins, victims, heros . . . , the text incorporates and makes them equal in value: Cain-Abel, Agamemnon, Cassandra, Socrates, Brutus, Moctezuma, Robespierre, Churruca, Lincoln, Trotsky, Madero, . . . Closely woven allusions in which each of the characters contributes their visible touch, constituting a dramatic, bloody altarpiece. Voices and shouts are heard including the one on "Friday afternoon"—possibly

God complaining of being forsaken.

The meditation on time, based on historical incident and myth, is like a deep structure under whose fluid framework it reveals itself. That the meditation is selective and crystallizes in an anthology of images as well as anecdotes is something good for poetry: Robespierre with his jaw broken carried to the guillotine; Churruca dying in Trafalgar with his smashed leg in a barrel of flour; Lincoln's, Trotsky's, Madero's, assassins synthesized in an instant, in one gesture. Thus the Poet declares his belligerency, his assumption of a moral attitude, very precise and convincing of course, safe for those who put truth ahead of dogma. The past is part of the present: yesterday's crimes are happening now and will happen tomorrow; that's why the lyrical voice asks (itself?): "doesn't anything happen as time passes?" and it (or the other) responds:

> —no pasa nada, sólo un parpadeo
> del sol, un movimiento apenas, nada,
> . . .
> los muertos están fijos en su muerte
> y no pueden morirse de otra muerte,
> . . .
> su muerte ya es la estatua de su vida
> un siempre estar ya nada para siempre,
> cada minuto es nada para siempre
> . . .
>
> (—nothing happens, just a blinding
> of the sun, hardly a movement, nothing
> . . .
> the dead are fixed in their death,
> and cannot die any other death,
> . . .
> their death is already the statue of their life,
> endless being and nothingness forever
> each minute is nothingness forever).

Nothing, death, forever, the irreversible declared insistently. The form of speech responds to the aesthetic necessity of preserving the moment in all the intensity of experience and at the same time sharing the moment with a continuity that fulfills the difficult paradox of absorbing and enhancing it. If memory is capricious, its whims were not arbitrary here but answers to the call of a consciousness which, as in "Espacio," is simultaneously the setting and agent of representation. Images, figures, forms of oblivion, all evoked by the poetic consciousness, which receives and plunges these images into currents, guiding them in such a way that yesterday's occurrences will continue flowing in the word which draws them up in a superior sphere of the same consciousness.

The poem nears its end as the ontological question is answered: I am who I am when I recognize myself in others, from them I receive the fullness of existence and to them I return it. Héloïse, Persephone, Mary—three women, three figures, who are one: astonishing and immortal woman, lover, mother, of a thousand faces, who takes us by her hand to the most secret of kingdoms. And the song of a never ending beginning: the last six lines of *Piedra de sol* are the same as the first six. This end is a beginning: the circle closes and the poem again unfolds the chain of propositions as if neither author nor reader are able to escape its fascination. Under the skin of the poem is heard the furious beat of Octavio Paz's heart.

trans. from the Spanish by Kosrof Chantikian

☆   ☆   ☆

José Miguel Oviedo

THE PASSAGES OF MEMORY:
READING A POEM BY OCTAVIO PAZ

Seremos lo que somos.
Borges: Swedenborg
(We will be what we are.)

In mid-1975 Octavio Paz published a poem called *Pasado en claro*[1] *(Past in Clarity)* written at the end of 1974 in Mexico and the United States. It's undoubtedly one of Paz's most important poetic works in practically a decade—assuming that *El mono gramático (The Monkey Grammarian,* 1974) is not strictly a poem, but rather an essay-poem—a criticism of the poem instead of the poem itself. Not only is it the longest poem Paz has written up till now, but it is an unfolding of a creative force comparable to his other great poems such as *Piedra de sol (Sun Stone,* 1957), *Viento entero (Wind from Every Compass Point,* 1965) or *Blanco* (1967).

But there is something more in which a part of its originality lies: it is the most confessional and moving poem that has come out of his hands, the most lyrical inquiry consistent with his origins, his personal past, his intellectual formation, his relation with Mexico, universal culture and above all, with himself—that elusive image he proposed fervently to grasp from the beginning of his poetic activity—a task always beginning for the first time, a task never ending. As regards an answer to the essential question—*Who am I really?*—this poem is a spiritual interpretation, a great poem of self-recognition, a process at once painful and consoling, tentative and urgent, obscure and lucid. Next to *Pasado en claro,* Paz's other poems in which he asks the same question seem merely rhapsodic and fragmentary. Here, at last, we have the agony of a search in its complete unfolding: the entire poem is an arrow the Poet fires at his own heart. The hunter is the quarry which

---

[1] Fondo de Cultura Económica: Mexico, 1975; [2nd revised ed. 1978. —Ed.] In what follows *Libertad bajo palabra* (Fondo de Cultura Económica: Mexico, 2nd ed., 1968) is abbreviated as *LBP.*

199

all his other masks had denied. Overwhelmed now with his discovery, he is by himself (with no one) and in this solitary companionship he communicates with himself and us through his own memory. Thus *Pasado en claro* questions by placing a probe into the past in order that yesterday may explain today and maybe even tomorrow.

The Footprint of Life

In Paz's poetic path there are various key instances connecting up with *Pasado en claro*, the most recent and perfect. Of the three major poems already mentioned, *Piedra de sol* turns out to be the most illustrious antecedent; by comparison with *Blanco* and *Viento entero*, it appears much more anchored on the level of experiences that can be identified and even dated. It is a masterful summary of universal human experiences, visions of the ancestral Mexican spirit and testimonies of some of the great events of our century reflected in the anguished consciousness of its creator. We recall that passage in which the evocation of individual steps leads us into the tragic memory of the Spanish Civil War:

> ¿comimos uvas en Bidart?, ¿compramos
> gardenias en Perote?,
>   nombres, sitios,
> calles y calles, rostros, plazas, calles,
> estaciones, un parque, cuartos solos,
> manchas en la pared, alguien se peina,
> alguien canta a mi lado, alguien se viste,
> cuartos, lugares, calles, nombres, cuartos,
>
> Madrid, 1937,
> en la Plaza del Ángel las mujeres
> cosían y cantaban con sus hijos,
> después sonó la alarma y hubo gritos,
> casas arrodilladas en el polvo,
> torres hendidas, frentes escupidas
> y el huracán de los motores, fijo:
>   (*LBP*, 245–46)

(Did we eat grapes in Bidart? Did we buy
gardenias in Perote?
                    names, places
streets and streets, faces, squares, streets,
train stations, a park, lonely rooms,
stains on a wall, someone combing their hair,
someone beside me singing, someone dressing,
rooms, places, streets, names, rooms,

Madrid 1937,
In the Plaza del Ángel women
were sewing and singing with their children
then the alarm sounded and there were screams,
houses cringing in the dust,
towers splitting, foreheads spat upon
and the hurricane of these engines, still:)

Pasado en claro picks up again the thread of these public
and private memories in a voice which had been lacking in
Paz's latest poetry. I refer to a voice which might be called
narrative, a result of evocations, scenes and ambience whose
accuracy of portrayal (or self-portrayal) does not want to be
overcome by the dialectical movement of the poem, but precisely remain. There is in that decision something so personal
from this poet whose elaborate images achieve a transcendent
flight above the data of the real world, that it is advisable to
observe it with care. (Of course, I am not equating the author
of the poem with the *I* who writes it. They may eventually
coincide but they are not the same. The former exists outside
the poem, the latter *only* within it.)

But even if that voice and that attitude had never been
more evident than in *Piedra de sol,* the latter is a very long
way from being the only antecedent that can be traced.
Throughout Paz's work, like a constant that comes and goes,
various poems detach themselves showing, though episodically,
the exploration of the profound waters of memory, the narrative mode and the confessional attitude. In "Cuarto de hotel" (Hotel Room), for example, the question was already being asked as it is again in *Pasado en claro:*

201

. . . ¿Lo que viví
lo estoy viviendo todavía?
¡Lo que viví! ¿Fui acaso? Todo fluye:
lo que viví lo estoy muriendo todavía.

(LBP, 75)

(. . . What I've lived
am I still living it?
What I've lived! Was I by chance? Everything flows:
I'm still dying of what I've lived.)

In another early poem similar to the first, "Elegía interrumpida" (Interrupted Elegy), memory is made to march by
". . . los muertos de mi casa" (. . . the dead of my house) like
"Rostros perdidos en mi frente" (LBP, 77) (Faces lost in my
head). In "El ausente" (The Absent One), he invokes his
people's blood and declares:

Por ti corro sediento
a través de mi estirpe,
hasta el pozo del polvo
donde mi semen se deshace en otros,
más antiguos, sin nombre,
ciegos ríos de cenizas y ruina.

(LBP, 95)

(Through you I run thirsty
through my ancestry,
to the well of dust
where my semen disappears in others,
older, nameless.
blind rivers of ashes and ruins.)

There are numerous memories of adolescence in various
places in ¿Águila o sol? (Eagle or Sun?) such as "Trabajos del
poeta" (Works of the Poet), "Un aprendizaje difícil" (A Difficult Apprenticeship), "Jardín con niño" (Garden with
Child), "Salida" (Way out) and so on. La estación violenta
(The Violent Season, 1958) contains a poem that constitutes
for me, along with Piedra de sol, the most direct antecedent
of Pasado en claro. It's called "¿No hay salida?" (Is There No

Way Out?) and is likewise an inquiry centered on the identity of an *I* which, in the middle of a nocturnal and threatening atmosphere, descends toward its own past and discovers it is a void, a time without time:

> toda la infancia se la tragó este instante y todo el porvenir
> son estos muebles clavados en su sitio

> (all childhood was swallowed by this instant and the
> whole future is this furniture nailed into its place)

The poem ends in the impasse alluded to by the title, the captive consciousness between sordid and nightmarish images:

> . . . todo está lejos, los
> muros son enormes,
> está a millas de distancia el vaso de agua, tardaré mil años en
> recorrer mi cuarto,
> qué sonido remoto tiene la palabra vida, no estoy aquí, no hay
> aquí, este cuarto está en otra parte,
> aquí es ninguna parte, poco a poco me he ido cerrando y no
> encuentro salida que no dé a este instante,
> este instante soy yo, salí de pronto de mí mismo, no tengo
> nombre ni rostro,
> yo estoy aquí, echado a mis pies, mirándome mirándose mirarme
> mirado.
>
> *(LBP, 228–29)*

> (. . . everything is far away, the
> walls are enormous,
> that glass of water is miles away, I will take a thousand years
> to cross my room,
> what a remote sound the word life has, I'm not here, there is
> no here, this room is somewhere else,
> here is nowhere, little by little I have been shutting myself in
> and I find no way out that doesn't give into this instant,
> I am this instant, I left myself suddenly, I haven't a
> name nor a face,
> I am here, thrown at my feet, looking at myself looking at
> himself to see myself looked at.)

But these passages, as well as the retrospective flashes that cross the body of *Piedra de sol* like lightning, the

> . . . corredores sin fin de la memoria
>
> (*LBP*, 239)

(. . . corridors of endless memory),

the familiar

> . . . miradas que nos ven desde el principio
>
> (*LBP*, 244)

(. . . looks that see us from the outset),

the groping along

> . . . por las calles de mí mismo
>
> (*LBP*, 249)

(. . . through the byways of myself)

—are merely elements that *Pasado en claro* is going to definitively organize almost twenty years later. Definitive in the sense of being integral and established in a work of art of unusual intensity and perception.

The Poetic System

Pasado en claro has 628 lines* (*Piedra de sol* 584). The rhythm is basically an alternation of 7, 9, and 11 syllable verses though there are more than a few alexandrines. Its rotation isn't regular but it keeps a very close and above all, a very harmonic relation with the idea of the poem. The pace of the text is also very harmonic. It is a sort of mental journey, the crossing of the *I* toward itself along thirteen stages or episodes.[2]

---

*The second revised edition of *Pasado en claro* (1978) contains 605 lines. J. M. Oviedo's article, published in 1976 and therefore based on the first edition, contains some verses Paz has transformed or eliminated from the second edition; conversely, certain verses present in the second edition do not exist in the first edition. In the pages that follow, Oviedo's quotations of *Pasado en claro*, where possible, have been made to conform to the later 1978 edition —Ed.

[2] It may be relevant to recall that the number 13 seems to exert a particular fascination for Paz. *Piedra de sol* has an epigraph from Nerval that begins:

> La Treizième revient . . . C'est encor la première;

Its symbolism is known from the Tarot cards—representing death or resurrection after death.

The initially dark atmosphere, the confusion of embarking on the journey, are all overcome after a series of dramatic incidents, in a vision of clarity and knowledge. But this triumph rests on a defeat. The *I* proves that it is only the shadow of a verbal reality, a voice that emerges from emptiness searching for someone. At the end of the poem, this consciousness is extinguished and it dissolves in silence, in nothingness. All this displacement is free and at the same time precise because it is mounted on a flexible system of correspondences, analogies and oppositions, of advances and regressions, of brilliant visions and echoes of these visions. There are at least three pairs of elements that constitute a kind of figure or *pattern* to which the text always flows back:

AIR – FIRE
WATER – EARTH
DARKNESS – LIGHT

These three pairs in their turn, reveal another three, which constitute the same elements but which are transcended and incarnated in images:

REALITY – WRITING
MEMORY – PRESENT
PASSION – KNOWLEDGE

In this way they form a sign, a *hexagram,* in which each unity has an absolute value yet is also relative since their possible combinations are many. It is a single sign but in movement. As poetic theory and practice, this method based on the *I Ching* has been used by Paz. In his prologue to the well-known anthology *Poesía en movimiento (Poetry in Movement),* Paz explains:

> Aplicar los signos del movimiento a una situación en movimiento es más fácil que tratar de entenderla con categorías y conceptos inmóviles. . . . En realidad, para mí no es método: es un juego. Como todos los juegos, obedece a leyes precisas. Como casi ningún otro juego, estimula la percepción y la imaginación.

> (Applying the signs of movement to a situation in movement is much easier than trying to comprehend it with

static categories and concepts. . . . In fact, for me it's not a methodology: it's a game. And like all games, it obeys precise laws. But like almost no other game, this one stimulates our perception and imagination.)[3]

The structure of *Pasado en claro* is then, the result of these movements and mutations, of a changing system interlacing all 628 lines.

The parts in which this system unfolds are rather well marked in the poem. The first (lines 1–20) unleashes a preliminary movement of initiation and search that culminates in the middle of the second stage. Actually, it contains a double movement: spreading out and falling back. The poem has an epigraph by Wordsworth:

> Fair seed-time had my soul, and I grew up
> Foster'd alike by beauty and by fear

that announces with precision the climate with which the text opens: a soul pursued by the solitary question of its origins. In the very first lines of the poem this soul is absorbed: it listens to the murmur of the past, the "mental steps" which memory wants to identify in the gloomy chaos that surrounds it. It hears (and thinks it hears) the sound of someone walking but

> . . . los pasos pasan
> hacia lugares que se vuelven aire
>
> (. . . the steps move
> toward places where they become air)

—echoes of emptiness. It's the idea he expressed with dramatic concentration in the poem "Aquí" (Here) in *Salamandra*:

> Mis pasos en esta calle
> Resuenan
>   En otra calle
> Donde
>   Oigo mis pasos
> Pasar en esta calle
> Donde

---

[3] Siglo XXI: Mexico, 4th ed. 1970, p. 25.

Sólo es real la niebla

(My steps on this street
Resound
        In another street
Where
      I hear my steps
Passing on this street
Where

Only the fog is real.)

Air is a key word. It alludes to the spirit of nature and the
creative force of the poetic word. The past is reduced to the
names of the past: words without sense, objects lost among
the ruins. Suddenly, for the first time, light beats down on
that barren land:

El sol camina sobre los escombros
de lo que digo, el sol arrasa los parajes
confusamente apenas
amaneciendo en esta página,
el sol abre me frente,
              balcón al voladero
dentro de mí.

(The sun moves among the rubble
of what I'm saying, the sun
beats down on these places invisibly
hardly dawning on this page
the sun opens my forehead
              balcony to the cliff
within myself.)

The contrast between the first thirteen lines and the last
seven is very sharp. The sullen confusion and deadly feeling
of stagnation (as in "Is There No Way Out?") leads to a solar
vision that illuminates the debris of reality, makes that other
reality—the text—dawn and finally clears away the fog from
consciousness. Even visually the eighteenth and nineteenth
lines suggest, with their alliterations and the gap they leave

between themselves, that attitude of opening toward the unknown and unlimited space: "balcony to the cliff."

The twenty-first line ("Me alejo de mí mismo"—I move away from myself) marks the articulation of the first movement with the second stage of the poem (lines 21–67). We are at the moment of unfolding: the *I* hurls itself into an abyss trying to catch up with itself. The poet launches his first probe into the waters of the past in order to recapture his true image. In the abstract setting previously outlined, some feature begins to define itself: "senda de piedras y de cabras" (trail of stones and goats). The eyes begin to see overwhelmed by the dazzling light

> Desde mi frente salgo a un mediodía
> del tamaño del tiempo
>
> (From my forehead I go out into a midday
> as large as time),

while words attempt to put in order and express a thought that splits "between the premonition and the meaning." Imagination and experience, intuition and perception: the search is nourished by contradictory efforts and contrary tensions that appear to annul it. The *I* decides to choose that rational stumbling block:

> Ni allá ni aquí: por esa linde
> de duda, transitada
> sólo por espejos y vislumbres,
> donde el lenguaje se desdice,
> voy al encuentro de mí mismo.
>
> (Neither over there nor here: through that boundary
> of doubt, passing
> only through glimmers and mirages
> where language withdraws
> I go to meet myself.)

That falling inside is a falling inside of language: the past also lives in it. Announced by "glimmers and mirages" it is quickly bathed in the pure light of line 48:

La hora es bola de cristal

(Time is a crystal ball).

We are in the vertical time always present in Paz's poetry,
that solar and carnal midday that lasts an eternity of a moment. And we enter in this way into the first physical abode
recorded (invented) by memory: the patio, with its garden
and its rustle of trees. A perfect ritual scenery if we recall the
beginning of *Piedra de sol*.[4] The same symbolic fusion of
vegetable and liquid is here (the ash and the well of water),
but intensified; all the meanings and elements are joined in
lines 51–53, where there is a Quevedian resonance:

> El fresno, sinüosa llama líquida,
> es un rumor que se levanta
> hasta volverse torre hablante

> (The ash, sinuous liquid flame,
> is a murmur that rises up
> until it becomes a speaking tower).

This announces another transition: the element Water (the
vital forces, the superior existence of consciousness) merges,
literally pours itself into the element Earth (the arid and inert,
the lower world) and converts it to a fluid space:

> Estoy dentro del ojo: el pozo
> donde desde el principio un niño
> está cayendo, el pozo donde cuento

---

[4] un sauce de cristal, un chopo de agua,
un alto surtidor que el viento arquea,
un árbol bien plantado mas danzante,
un caminar de río que se curva,
avanza, retrocede, da un rodeo
y llega siempre

(a willow of crystal, a poplar of water
a high gushing fountain curved by the wind
a tree well planted but dancing
a movement of river waters which curves
advances, recedes, makes a detour
and always arrives).
   (LBP, 237)

lo que tardo en caer desde el principio,
el pozo de la cuenta de mi cuento
por donde sube el agua y baja
mi sombra.

(I am inside the eye: the well
where from the outset a boy is falling,
the well where I recount
how long it takes me to fall from the outset
the well of the recounting of my story
from which water rises and
my shadow falls).

New descent, much closer to the bottom still; these lines
ending the second stage warn us that the limits of that past
may be unreachable. As in a bad dream, the child continues
falling, is falling right now—pursuing his shadow.

The Mexican Fire

The third stage goes from line 68 to 99. The key element here is Fire. The first line is a summary of the elements
presented in the last section ("the patio, the wall, the ash, the
well") that resolve themselves "in a clarity in the form of a
lake." The expansion of the element Water symbolizes of
course, the origin of Mexico, its mythic past and turbulent
history. The *I* now sails through waters that take it to a reunion with its people and its collective destiny:

entre el cielo y la tierra,
una piragua solitaria.
Las olas hablan nahua

(between sky and earth
a solitary piragua.
The waves speak Nahuatl).

Appearing unexpectedly then, the contrary, Fire; first there
is a "foreshadowing of a brazier" and then a raging flame, a
great fire that devastates everything in a huge catastrophe:

La luz poniente se demora,
alza sobre la alfombra simétricos incendios,
vuelve llama quimérica
este volumen lacre que hojeo
(estampas: los volcanes, los cúes y, tendido,
manto de plumas sobre el agua,
Tenochtitlán todo empapado en sangre).
Los libros del estante son ya brasas
que el sol atiza con sus manos rojas.
Se rebela mi lápiz a seguir el dictado.
En la escritura que la nombra
se eclipsa la laguna.

(The sunset light lingers on,
rising symmetrical fires over the carpet
turning this red book I leaf through
into an illusionary flame
(engravings: volcanos, ancient temples and
a cloak of feathers spread out above the water
Tenochtitlán everywhere drenched in blood).
The books from the shelf are now embers
the sun stirs up with its red hands.
My pencil rebels against continuing this dictation.
In the writing which names it
the lake is overshadowed.)

Water has undergone a transformation. Now it is blood, "liquid flame"—that which springs up from the sacrificial stone
(the brazier, the flint) and from the crimes of the conquest
(the cross, Tenochtitlán). The pure and transparent colors
that we began to see in the second stage, have turned to mor-
bid, incarnating and violent tones. Blood inundates the Mexican lake; reading ("this red volume that I leaf through") para-
lyzes the writing that was motivating ("My pencil rebels
against continuing this dictation"). The vision is disturbed
and founders in an impasse. "Doblo la hoja" (I turn the leaf)
indicates the beginning of another introduction. The phrase
has at least two meanings: the leaf of paper and the leaf of a
plant. We are always in a landscape of words:

cuchicheos:
me espían entre los follajes
de las letras.

(whispers:
spy on me among the foliage
of letters.)

We have fallen into a place very similar to the beginning, whispers, steps, echoes. The signals reaching the poet from his past are uncertain and confused. The unraveling of the plot must continue.

The Puddle and Thirst

The fourth stage (lines 100–126) constitutes another turning point in the depths of memory that still resists illumination. The lake of blood is now a puddle, a well of shadows:

Un charco es mi memoria.
Lodoso espejo: ¿dónde estuve?
Sin piedad y sin cólera mis ojos
me miran a los ojos
desde las aguas turbias de ese charco
que convocan ahora mis palabras.

(My memory is a puddle.
Muddy mirror: where was I?
Merciless and without anger my eyes
look me in the eye
from the cloudy waters of this pond
that now summon my words.)

The first question—*where was I?*—is going to be the central theme of this section (appearing three times) that comes and goes between the *puddle* of memory and the ambiguous *mirror* of words. Slowly, floating on both, the poet begins to comprehend:

No veo con los ojos: las palabras
son mis ojos. Vivimos entre nombres;
lo que no tiende nombre todavía
no existe: *Adán de lodo,*

no un muñeco de barro, una metáfora.
Ver al mundo es deletrearlo.

(I do not see with my eyes: words
are my eyes. We live among names;
what hasn't a name
doesn't exist: *Adam of mud,*
not a clay doll, a metaphor.
To see the world is to decipher it.)

That harsh mental conquest has its correspondences in
the passage from past to present, from experience to the writing. From line 114 on these passages are going to be expressed
in images that oppose the darkness of the puddle to an indecisive light and the sensation of thirst and aridity to the vora-
ciousness of reading:

Brillan,
entre enramadas de reflejos,
nubes varadas y burbujas
sobre un fondo del ocre al brasilado,
las sílabas de agua.

(Syllables of water
sparkle in reflected branches,
stranded clouds and bubbles
over a background of
ochre and brazilred.)

The traditional idea in which one can have "reading-thirst"
and in which reading satisfies spiritual necessities lies at the
bottom of these admirable lines:

Mis ojos tienen sed. El charco es senequista:
el agua, aunque potable, no se bebe: se lee.
Al sol del altiplano se evaporan los charcos.

(My eyes are thirsty. The puddle is wise
the water, though drinkable, is not drunk—it is read.
The puddles evaporate in the high plateau sun.)

A new dialectical movement: the sun (of knowledge, of

213

the Mexican plateau) dries up the puddle in that "disloyal dust" leaving things that can be *read:*

unos cuantos vestigios intestados

(a few unwilled vestiges).[5]

The implication that what remains is a personal legacy or treasure (a legacy of dust) is very clear and functions as an incitement to inquire into it with greater eagerness.

The Fig Tree from the Past

The fifth stage is the longest of the poem (lines 127–208) and begins with a resounding affirmation:

Yo estoy en donde estuve

(I am where I was).

The *I* perceives the real past never *existed;* it *exists,* rather, like a persistent re-creation of the Imagination. Time, therefore, is an illusion: yesterday is here and will be tomorrow. Every past is the same, is that instant in which we visit the same "patio of words." Memory flows like a bunch of personal and strange recollections jumbled all together:

Abderramán, Pompeyo, Xicoténcatl,
batallas en el Oxus o en la barda
con Ernesto y Guillermo . . .

---

[5] Compare these lines with those from "Maithuna" which play with the same idea of verbal drought:

Hora vertical
　　　La sequía
Mueve sus ruedas espejeantes
Jardín de navajas
　　　　　Festín de falacias
(Vertical time
　　　The drought
Moves its gleaming wheels
Garden of razors
　　　　　Feast of deceitfulness)

Ladera este (Joaquín Mortiz: Mexico, 3rd ed. 1975), p. 117.

(Abd-ar-Rahman, Pompeii, Xicoténcatl,
battles in the Oxus or in the brambles
with Ernesto and Guillermo . . .).

There is a violent proximity of characters from a remote
civilization and history to a youthful memory; an atmosphere
of intimacy is created with the names Ernesto and Guillermo.
And at this point a decisive symbolic element surges forth in
the process that describes this poem:

. . . La mil hojas
verdinegra escultura del murmullo,
jaula del sol y la centella
breve del chupamirto: la higuera primordial . . .

(. . . The thousand leaves,
darkgreen sculpture of whispers,
cage of the sun and lightning
quickness of the hummingbird: the primordial fig tree . . .)

The century old fig tree is the image *par excellence* of
that which endures: presence of the past, revocation of time
in permanence. It is an image familiar to readers of Paz's
poetry. In *¿Águila o sol?* there is a prose poem called "The
Fig Tree," in which this tree appears tied to memories of
adolescence. The sight of the fig tree sets off a furiously im-
passioned reflection concerning *to have been, to be now,* and
the future *not to be:*

. . . Adolescencia feroz: el hombre que quiere ser, y que
ya no cabe en ese cuerpo demasiado estrecho, estrangula
al niño que somos. (Todavía, al cabo de los años, el que
voy a ser, y que no será nunca, entra a saco en el que
fui, arrasa mi estar, lo deshabita, malbarata riquezas,
comercia con la Muerte.) Pero en ese tiempo la higuera
llegaba hasta mi encierro y tocaba insistente los vidrios
de la ventana, llamándome.

(. . . Ferocious adolescence: the man who wants to be,
and who can no longer fit in that very tight body,

strangles the child whom we are. (Still, after all the
years, what I'm going to be, but never will be, plunders
who I was, ravages my being, depopulates it, squanders
riches, has dealings with Death.) But in those days the
fig tree reached up to my cell and persistently knocked
against my window, calling me.)

There is another poem, earlier still, entitled "The Shadow,"
in which the fig tree swells with a secret sexual symbolism:

> . . . Higuera maternal:
> la cicatriz del tronco, entre las hojas,
> era una boca hambrienta, femenina,
> viva en la primavera. . . .
> *(LBP, 71)*

> (. . . Motherly fig tree:
> the scar of the trunk between the leaves
> was a hungry mouth, feminine,
> alive in the spring. . . .)

The image of the fig tree in these poems coincides reveal-
ingly with that in *Pasado en claro,* even on the level of the
scenographic details that accompany it: the wall, the greenness, nature's spring gust. The idea of plant persistence recurs
in other ways: in *Piedra de sol* we find

> un sauce de cristal, un chopo de agua

> (a willow of crystal, a poplar of water)

and in *El mono gramático* we find ourselves with venerable
trees like that

> gran baniano que debe ser viejísimo a juzgar por
> el número de sus raíces colgantes y la forma
> intrincada en que descienden a la tierra desde lo alto
> de la copa
>
> (p. 31)

> (great brahman who must be very old judging by the
> number of his hanging roots and the intricate way

they fall to earth from the top of the crown),

the same as fleetingly appears at the start of this poem

> El asalto de siglos del baniano
> contra la vertical paciencia de la tapia

> (the centuries old assault of the brahman
> against the vertical patience of that adobe wall),

or the confused tangle of trees and vegetables in which appears

> la higuera religiosa a cuya sombra el Buda venció
> a Mara

> (the religious fig tree in whose shadow the Buddha
> defeated Mara).

Sacred tree, but also malignant and cursed (the infernal fig tree—biblical instrument of Judas' damnation), this element is linked in the poem to the notions of transgression and blame. The fig tree is witness to the awakening of the senses, the irruption in Paz's poetry of that intense reality, the Body and its eroticism:

> capilla vegetal de ritüales
> polimorfos, diversos y perversos.
> Revelaciones y abominaciones:
> el cuerpo y sus lenguajes
> entretejidos, nudo de fantasmas
> palpados por el pensamiento
> y por el tacto disipados,
> argolla de la sangre, idea fija
> en mi frente clavada

> (vegetal chapel of polymorphic, diverse
> and depraved rituals
> Revelations and abominations:
> the body and its interlacing languages
> phantom bond touched by thought
> and dissipated by a touch,
> ring of blood, obsession
> nailed to my forehead).

The pregnant atmosphere, the heavy and remorseful sensuality of these lines dissolve in a sensation of unreality: the *I* fades away in a sea of desire:

> El deseo es señor de espectros
> el deseo nos vuelve espectros

> (Desire is the lord of ghosts
> desire turns us into ghosts).

Everything becomes phantom-like and burns under his incandescent flow:

> yo fui la enredadera imaginaria

> (I was the imaginary bindweed).

But that void opens another reality behind "reality": the plenitude of nothingness. The image of the fig tree returns to the poem transfigured as something else: as in "The Shadow," it is a sex, a throbbing crevice, a promise of intimate pleasure:

> La hendedura del tronco:
> sexo, sello, pasaje serpentino
> cerrado al sol y a mis miradas,
> abierto a las hormigas.

> (The crevice in the trunk:
> sex, seal, winding passage
> closed to the sun and my looks
> open to the ants.)

The limits disappear: a wave of joy spreads, of clarity and incarnated vitality. The poetry celebrates this *fiesta:* the day

> prorrumpe entre las hojas

> (bursts out among the leaves);

> El tiempo es luz filtrada

> (Time is light leaking out):

from the fig tree

>   escurre savia lechosa y acre

>   (milky and tart sap discharges);

in that world beyond the obvious

>   son verdes las mareas
>   la sangre es verde, el fuego verde,
>   entre las yerbas negras arden estrellas verdes

>   (the tides are green,
>   the blood is green, the fire green,
>   among the black grasses green stars burn);

there is, finally, an orgy of sensations:

>   son ojos las yemas de los dedos,
>   el tacto mira, palpan las miradas,
>   los ojos oyen los olores

>   (our fingertips are eyes,
>   the touch sees, the looks throb
>   the eyes hear the smells).

That *other-reality* is presented in the lines that follow as something enchanted, like a kingdom of wonders

>   hay una reina diminuta
>   en un país de musgo desterrada

>   (there is a tiny queen exiled
>   in a country of moss).

but always dominated by a sexual impulse, whose violence gives origin to aggressive images like the

>   agua que perfora
>   la vetas espirales

>   (water that pierces
>   the spiral veins)

and afterwards hurls itself

219

por unos labios entreabietos

(through half-open lips),

or the

ríos de cuchillos que nunca desembocan

(rivers of knives that never end).

The erotic urgency inverts the sense of its force. Desire previously annuled the *I*—now an *I* of "greedy fingers" outlives desire. New ebb toward the well of memories that those very fingers want to detain. But the

horas de arena fluyen hacia un sin donde tácito
—no hay escuelas allá dentro,
siempre es el mismo día, siempre la misma noche,
no han inventado el tiempo todavía,
no ha envejecido el sol,
esta nieve es idéntica a la yerba,
siempre y nunca es lo mismo,
nunca ha llovido y llueve siempre,
todo está siendo y nunca ha sido

(hours of sand flow toward an unspoken nowhere
—there are no schools inside
it's always the same day, always the same night
time hasn't been invented yet
the sun hasn't aged
this snow is the same as grass
always and never are the same
it has never rained here and it always rains
everything is becoming and nothing has ever been).

Memories exist, but they're no one's, they flutter like a transparency no one can take and identify as their own: they are "names in search of bodies." The fig tree has confused the poetic consciousness (the text will speak of it again, of its "deceits and wisdom"), because everything changes and to cling to immobility is a gross error. There are no fig trees, there are simply perceptions of a fig tree and words that say "fig tree." We move among apparitions and illusions, like another illusion; we talk with ghosts and are able

> hablar con vivos y con muertos.
> También conmigo mismo.

> (to talk with the living and the dead.
> Even with myself.)

We have reached the end of the fifth stage and we receive a profound lesson: if the past invents the *I*, what is able to stop the past from becoming plural, a point of discovery and communion of many live, dead, imagined voices? This unfolding is the material of the following stage.

The Delirium of Books

The sixth stage is a dialogue between the elements Air and Fire, the other signs of the hexagram: between the knowledge that illuminates and the dark vertigo of passion. The light, flimsy nature of the first lines is apparent: "espacios diáfanos (diaphanous spaces), "El cielo es giratorio lapiz-lázuli" (The sky is a revolving lapis lazuli), "la luz se precipita de las cumbres" (light hurls itself down from the summits). But just before a fusion point has been produced: "llamas entre las nieves de las nubes" (flames among the snow of clouds) and then the limits of light are pointed out: "la sombra se derrama por el llano" (the shadow spreads throughout the plain). Light and fire, lights and shadows: in fact, now it is another light, one which illuminates the night of secretly read books in the house of childhood:

> A la luz de la lámpara—la noche
> ya dueña de la casa y el fantasma
> de mi abuelo ya dueño de la noche—
> yo penetraba en el silencio,
> cuerpo sin cuerpo, tiempo
> sin horas. Cada noche,
> máquinas transparentes del delirio,
> dentro de mí los libros levantaban
> arquitecturas sobre una sima edificadas.

221

(By the lamp's light—the night
now mistress of the house and the ghost
of my grandfather now lord of the night—
I penetrated into the silence,
body without body, time
without hours. Each night those books,
transparent machines of delirium,
built within me structures
hanging over an abyss.)

This emotional memory of the formative books of his
first years is going to occupy all the rest of this stage. It is
probably the fragment in which Paz has left more personal
clues and signs scattered: at times his poem is a palimpsest
running through dates, paraphrases and homages to his favor-
ite authors and books. To celebrate these presences which he
summons, Paz lights a communal fire:

Yo junté leña con los otros
y lloré con el humo de la pira

(I collected firewood with the others
and cried with the pyre's smoke).

Sounds and echos soon flow of memories of Garcilaso ("que
arrastra el Tajo turbiamente verde"), of Góngora ("la líquida
espesura se encrespaba/tras de la fugitiva Galatea"), Nerval ("in
the cavern I swam with the siren"), Dante, Villaurrutia, Verne
("the octopus and Nemo") and many others. This collection
of readings is marked by erotic fire: "the taut body, the intense look." That high temperature gives a soothing and re-
freshing fruit, whose name we are not told but which we intuit:

Nombres anclados en el golfo
de mi frente: yo escribo porque el druida,
bajo el rumor de sílabas del himno,
encina bien plantada en una página,
me dio el gajo de muérdago, el conjuro
que hace brotar palabras de la peña.

(Names anchored in the gulf

of my forehead: I write because the druid,
under the murmur of the hymn's syllables,
holm oak well planted on a page,
gave me the mistletoe branch, the incantation
that makes words sprout up from the rock.)

This magic trophy can be none other than that very
Poetry, revealing, purifying and fertile force: Water over
Earth. It is not strange therefore, that his emblems should be
the holm oak ("well planted" says the line repeating one of
the incantatory formulas of *Piedra de sol)* and the mistletoe
of the Celtic poetry, and that this pair Earth-Water refers
again to the element Air: "Adolescence, country of clouds"
on ending this stage.

House of the Dead

The pathos and pain that rip through the seventh stage
are the most intense of the entire poem because they follow
upon an important discovery: memory dances with Death,
that is, with the dead. There is no abstraction here: the dead
have names, they are (for the *I) its* dead, *its* blood. The recol-
lection focuses on a familiar home:

> Casa grande
> encallada en un tiempo
> azolvado
>
> (Large house
> foundering in time
> becoming clogged).

Becoming clogged alludes to the darkness that obstructs the
flow of memory. It means "blocking up a channel"; that
house occupies the same gloomy place where the poem begins.
The details are recovered one by one and the description
reaches a geographic precision: "the huge trees," "the dwarf-
like church," "the little magenta shop," "the hawthorns and
the mandarins," the "wheel of Santa Catalina," all sketch a
familiar landscape. But that atmosphere overlooks emptiness.
It is inhabited solely by death and "the rancor of ancestors."
In that house, in the midst of those bitter evocations like

223

"scorpion beds," the poet recaptures his image as a child. The rancor and sorrow

> como a los perros dan con la pitanza
> vidrio molido

> (like those dogs to whom pulverized glass
> is fed with the leftovers),

are mixed—and this is what gives the passage its tormented tone—with affectionate memory and human pity. Four personages are outlined with clarity among the shadows of memory: the mother, aunt, grandfather and father. Let us turn once again to *Piedra de sol* where there is a previous indication of this searching study of loved ones, seen essentially like a collection of

> miradas enterradas en un pozo,
> miradas que nos ven desde el principio,
> mirada niña de la madre vieja
> que ve en el hijo grande un padre joven,
> mirada madre de la niña sola
> que ve en el padre grande un hijo niño,
> miradas que nos miran desde el fondo
> de la vida y son trampas de la muerte.
>
> *(LBP, 244)*

> (looks buried in a well,
> looks that from the outset see us,
> the girlish look of an old mother
> that sees a young father in the big son,
> the motherly look of a lonely girl
> that sees in her eminent father a little boy,
> looks that look into us from the very depths
> of life and are the traps of death.)

The list of dead is more explicit and detailed in *Pasado en claro*: each one of the four figures has carved their verbal niche and finished their last portrait in the poem. The mother is

    ... niña de mil años,
    madre del mundo, huérfana de mí,
    abnegada, feroz, obtusa, providente,
    jilguera, perra, hormiga, jabalina,
    carta de amor con faltas de lenguaje,
    mi madre: pan que yo cortaba
    con su propio cuchillo cada día.

    (... a thousand year old child,
    mother of the world, but devoid of me,
    self-sacrificing, ferocious, hard, prudent,
    goldfinch, bitch, ant, wild boar,
    love letter in poor language,
    my mother: bread that I used to cut
    with her own knife every day.)

The aunt appears like a somnambulant virgin who

    me enseñó a ver con los ojos cerrados

    (taught me to see with my eyes closed);

the grandfather who taught him

    sonreír en la caída
    y a repetir en los desastres: *al hecho, pecho*

    (to smile in falling
    and in disasters to repeat: *don't cry over spilt milk)*

is the addressee of an homage making use of Quevedo's words:

    Esto que digo es tierra
    sobre tu nombre derramada: *blanda te sea*

    (This which I say is earth
    scattered over your name: *may it be gentle to you).*

The father is the most terrible and convulsed figure of his gallery of dead: we see him "bound to the torture of alcohol"
coming and going "among the flames" and above all, cut off

    225

from his son. Only the dialogue of their solitude remains:

> Yo nunca pude hablar con él.
> Lo encuentro ahora en sueños,
> esa borrosa patria de los muertos.
> Hablamos siempre de otras cosas.
>
> (I was never able to talk with him.
> Now I find him in my dreams,
> that blurred country of the dead.
> We always talk of other things.)

The *I* feels it is barely a survivor, a tumorous outgrowth of these dead:

> yerba, maleza,
> entre escombros anónimos.
>
> (grass, weeds,
> among anonymous debris).

The Erotic Possession of the World

The eighth stage covers lines 352–412. Although the motive of death is present here, its real theme is another one: the ascension of the Tantric path in order to understand himself and the world. Among other things, Tantric thought tells us that we recognize ourselves only through experience, taking the world in a sensual embrace, copulating with it, merging ourselves with it in "a total carnal and spiritual experience."[6]

True reality is a fusion of doubles (or halves: male and female), polar attraction that repeats itself on every scale like a universal principle. The *I* is therefore, a unity of contraries. It is the sum of two adversary elements (body/soul) that must be reconciled. This mystical path of rupture with the monist and motionless conception of the West has given birth to many of Paz's poems and has penetrated deeply his poetic doctrine.[7]

---

[6] *Conjunciones y disyunciones* (Joaquín Mortiz: Mexico, 1969), p. 65. Hereafter abbreviated as *CD*.

[7] On the influence of Tantric thought here, see E. J. Wilson "Vision, Ecstasy and Eastern Thought in the Poetry of Octavio Paz," *Symposium*, 29, no. 1–2 (Spring–Summer 1975), pp. 164–179.

Through the lines with which the passage begins, Paz puts us in a joyous climate of liberating revelation: after the monologue with the dead, his dialogue with himself, free finally of the bonds of time:

> Días
> como una frente libre, un libro abierto.
> No me multiplicaron los espejos
> codiciosos que vuelven
> cosas los hombres, número las cosas:

> (Days
> like a mind free, an open book.
> I was not increased by the greedy
> mirrors that turn
> people into things and things into numbers).

Notice that, as is characteristic in Paz, the mystical path does not assume a religious link with any established divinity; the search is directed to an absolute *human;* the "greedy mirrors" surely symbolizes that deceitful temptation that dries and alienates the transcendental impulse:

> ni mando ni ganancia. La santidad tampoco:
> el cielo para mí pronto fue un cielo
> deshabitado, una hermosura hueca
> y adorable.

> (neither power nor profit. Nor sainthood either:
> the sky quickly became for me an empty sky
> a hollow and adorable
> beauty.)

The refusals—to sainthood, to power, to wealth—keep adding up. The way is open, empty, at one's disposal. The senses awake and the bodies of the *I* and of the world unite in a cosmic embrace. Significantly, the symbols of Light and Water and the image of the fig tree reappear in this moment of ecstasy and collision:

> No me habló Dios entre las nubes;
> entre las hojas de la higuera

me habló el cuerpo, los cuerpos de mi cuerpo.
Encarnaciones instantáneas:
tarde lavada por la lluvia,
luz recién salida del agua . . .

(God did not speak to me among the clouds;
my body spoke to me, the bodies of my body,
among the leaves of this fig tree.
Instantaneous incarnations:
an afternoon washed by the rain
light newly rising from the water . . .).

Consciousness, which already knows time is illusory, now intends to leave its prison once and for all. The *I* listens, amazed, to its own throbbing and recognizes the universal rhythm in it. The prime yearning is for a great harmonious dissolution in which neither Time nor Self really exist:

—como si al fin el tiempo coincidiese
consigo mismo y yo con él,
como si el tiempo y sus dos tiempos
fuesen un solo tiempo
que ya no fuese tiempo, un tiempo
donde siempre es *ahora* y a todas horas *siempre,*
como si yo y mi doble fuesen uno
y yo no fuese ya.

(—as if time finally coincided
with itself and I with it,
as if time and its two times
were a single time
that was no longer time, a time
where always is *now* and at all times *always*
as if I and my double were one
and I were no longer.)

That same happiness and that same mystical conviction shine in *Piedra de sol:*

. . . no hay tiempo ya, ni muro: ¡espacio, espacio,
abre la mano, coge esta riqueza . . .!
(*LBP,* 247)

(. . . there is no longer any time, nor barrier: space, space
open your hand, seize this richness!

and further on:

> para que pueda ser he de ser otro,
> salir de mí, buscarme entre los otros
> *(LBP, 252)*

(so that I might be I must be someone else,
to get out of myself to search for myself among others).

This confirms fittingly what I pointed out before: no matter
how "personal" the poem seems, the *I* that speaks and medi-
tates and rejoices is not an individual voice isolated from the
world, but surely, the *voice of the world,* a poetry made by
everyone as Lautréamont wanted. The instrument of cosmic
possession is the body, but bodies are texts just like stars
(celestial bodies) that form constellations we can *read.* Poetry is a form of copulation: intensity and expansion, ecstasy and emptiness that alternate rhythmically. As Paz says:

la carne se hace verbo—y el verbo se despeña.

(flesh becomes verb—and the verb hurls itself down.)

The sequence of contrary movements that are integrated
and reconciled only to be again separated, is illuminated by a
brief passage that is one of the poem's most perfect and in
which the thread—the theme of death—is picked up again
from the last stage:

> La muerte es madre de las formas . . .
> El sonido, bastón de ciego del sentido:
> escribo *muerte* y vivo en ella
> por un instante. Habito su sonido:
> es un cubo neumático de vidrio,
> vibra sobre esta página,
> desaparece entre sus ecos.
>
> (Death is mother of forms . . .
> Sound, blind person's cane of sense:
> I write *death* and live inside of her

for an instant. I inhabit her sound:
it is a pneumatic glass cube,
it vibrates on this page,
and disappears among its echoes.)

Paradoxically, death is also the origin, the creative root.
It is reborn from itself like a work that resounds and "is alive."
Death is therefore, life, just as "water is fire."

More and more, until the end, this poem is a poem about
language (self-reflective, overturned by its own material and
critical of it) because outside of words, those "amphibious
creatures" that "bathe in fire, rest in air," nothing exists but
appearances. But the words weave an intricate verbal labyrinth, difficult to comprehend:

Están del otro lado. No las oigo, ¿qué dicen?
No dicen: hablan, hablan.

(They're from another world. I don't hear them,
    what are they saying?
They don't say: they speak, they speak.)

The journey of recognition goes on, in another region
now: memories have become language and their meaning must
be deciphered, made to tell us what they have to say.

In Order that Psyche May Shine

Language, linked to the element Air will be, in the following part (lines 413–442), the protagonist of a battle after
Light and against darkness. Alluding as much to that displacement as to the continuity of poetic narration, the *I* em-
barks upon this stage with the lines

Salto de un cuento a otro
por un puente colgante de once sílabas

(I jump from one story to another
by a suspension bridge of eleven syllables).

The expression *story* reminds us of the voluntary narration
that lies at the bottom of the poem and which encourages its

230

march. It also serves to tie this part, already advanced in the development, together with the beginning movements

> el pozo de la cuenta de mi cuento

> (the well of the recounting of my story),

and with the last ones

> cuentos distintos de la misma cuenta

> (distinct stories from the same account);

the language-air, magic inspiration, is an active agent of the consciousness that questions. Its force is sexual:

> es un tornillo que perfora montes,
> nadador en la mar brava del fuego
> es invisible surtidor de ayes,
> levanta a pulso dos océanos,
> anda perdido por las calles
> palabra en pena en busca de sentido,
> aire que se disipa en aire.

> (it is a screw that pierces mountains,
> swimmer in the wild sea of fire
> it is an invisible fountain of cries,
> lifts two oceans with its bare hands,
> walks through the streets lost
> sorrowful word in search of meaning,
> air which dissipates in air.)

But that luminous *spirit* again suffers the pursuit of shadows and inhuman violence. Suddenly, in that clear air of the word, night falls, a night illuminated by the moon:

> La *cabeza de muerto,* mensajera
> de las ánimas, la fascinante fascinada
> por las camelias y la luz eléctrica . . .

> (The *head of death,* messenger
> of souls, the fascinating fascinated
> by the camellias and electric light . . .).

This passage, which treats the famous cliché with a tone of somber fear possibly inspired in Lugones, is like a homage to the poets (in love with the moon) who officiate in the darkness without ever seeing light. There is a bloody rite: a request to kill the moon and burn her like a witch. Something new is born for the poet's entrancing contemplation from this sacrifice: "Light scattered, Psyche." The short fable seems like a reelaboration of a Greek myth: Psyche triumphs over Aphrodite's hate and purified by her own suffering, becomes immortal.

The result of the struggle is very uncertain and tightly binds the ninth and tenth stages together. That link is announced by the introduction: "Are there messengers? Yes," alluding to an epithet applied to the moon. But the theme which deals with the episode is of History as a language that speaks about and with us. This is also a struggle between darkness and Light—between, if you will, barbarism and human order. So that the language of history is a brutal shout leading to the fall and to death:

> El universo habla solo
> pero los hombres hablan con los hombres:
> hay historia. Guillermo, Alfonso, Emilio:
> el corral de los juegos era historia
> y era historia jugar a morir juntos.
> La polvareda, el grito, la caída:
> algarabía, no discurso.
>
> (The universe speaks alone
> but humans speak with humans:
> there is history. Guillermo, Alfonso, Emilio:
> the corral of games was history
> and to play at being dead together was history.
> The dust cloud, the scream, the fall:
> gibberish, not speech.)

History is at once a dimension devastated by the denying forces of human beings (ambition for power, treachery, lies) and a space where humankind painfully recognizes its condition of solidarity with its counterparts. We are bound to cyclic fluctuations between fratricide and compassion:

232

Ser tiempo es la condena, nuestra pena es la historia.
Pero también es el lugar de prueba:
reconocer en el borrón de sangre
del lienzo de Verónica la cara
del otro—siempre el otro es nuestra víctima.

(Our sentence is time's existence, our prison history.
But it is also the proving ground:
to recognize in the blotch of blood
on Veronica's handkerchief the face
of the other—the other is always our victim.)

Paz proposes an alternative: death might *not* be the exit
from history:

El escape, quizás, es hacia dentro

(Maybe the escape is inside)

toward where the pronouns of egotism and contempt dissolve.
Again reconciliation in a great whole associated with the rupture of temporal limits:

En el centro del tiempo ya no hay tiempo
es movimiento hecho fijeza, círculo
anulado en sus giros

(In the center of time there is no longer time
it is movement made stillness, circular
annulling in its turns.)

The Third Being

The eleventh part (lines 532–590) culminates a miraculous operation that has throughout been the poem's intention: memory, once and for all makes itself *presence,* instant fixed in this instant, revelation pure and total. The sexual union with the world reaches the movement of ecstasy: the vision of an absolute *blank* that destroys the appearance of things in a perfect immobility. In the hour that reigns over this carnal and mystical experience, light arises like a powerful fire that destroys the cloistering of memory. The walls tumble:

233

Entre muros—de piedra no:
por la memoria levantados—
transitoria arboleda:
luz reflexiva entre los troncos
y la respiración del viento.

(Between walls—not of stone:
lifted by memory—
transitory grove:
reflective light between the trunks
and the breathing of the wind.)

The deceptive surface of things fades away, the skies open and aerial energy flows:

el alma es ya, vacante, espacio puro

(the soul is already, vacant, pure space).

The world, in suspense, empties itself in being while being gives itself to the world: a maximum fusion proving that the *I* has reached the difficult "third state" which mystics speak of: Paz explains it as he lives it intensely:

Hay un estar tercero
el ser sin ser, la plenitud vacía,
hora sin horas y otros nombres
con que se muestra y se dispersa
en las confluencias del lenguaje
no la presencia: su presentimiento.
Los nombres que la nombran dicen: *nada,*
palabra de dos filos, palabra entre dos huecos.

(There is a third state:
being without being, a plenitude of emptiness,
time without hours and other names
with which it is shown and dispersed
in the confluence of language
not the presence: its premonition.
The names that name it say: *nothing,*
double-edged word, word between two openings.)

It is necessary to read with special care one of the lines of this last passage: "no la presencia: su presentimiento" (not the presence: its premonition) because in it is contained a fundamental idea of Paz's poetics. Language, like premonition, is divine: ("Is God") or a presence beyond our grasp, outside of the experience we call a poem. Poetry is a perpetual tension that aims toward that blank from which alone we have flashes, bursts. Through it reality reveals its genuine face—the face denied by evidence. Authentic knowledge is not the fruit of a fixed or predictable method. In another poem, "Lectura de John Cage" (Reading John Cage), Paz postulates a principle or paradox of Tantric thought:

> El saber no es saber:
> Recobrar la ignorancia,
> Saber del saber.

> (Knowledge is not knowing:
> To recover ignorance,
> Knowledge of knowing.)

In *Pasado en claro*, knowledge is found with a chance meeting:

> En las conversaciones con la higuera
> o entre los blancos del discurso

> (In talks with the fig tree
> or among the gaps of speech).

Each instance of confusion and delirium has opened the possibility of revelation: "en la conjuración de las imágenes" (in the conspiracy of images), in "el desvarío de las simetrías" (the delirium of symmetries) or in "el dudoso jardín de la memoria" (the uncertain garden of memory).

The sacred presence appears before it vanishes into other forms. It has neither shape nor body and for that reason alone, language, which is the metaphor of the body, is able to reveal it. Poetry joins and restores the world to us. Poetic activity, like this third state, is always a dissidence, a starting on the fringe in order to return to the lost center.

The Poetic Epiphany

The last two stages of the poem form a sequence through their close connection: the twelfth marks the end of the process of self-recognition and the last, very short, is really an epilogue that skillfully gathers together the leading threads of the poem: Memory and Present, merged in the splendid totality of poetry. In the penultimate section the poet makes a summary of his own voyage which has brought him from appearances to a vision of that "God with no body" or "word without any contrary." The summary is certainly self-critical and with an image of Borgesian flavor he laments about the paths that have made his journey drag on until finally:

Alcé con las palabras y sus sombras
una casa ambulante de reflejos

(I built a walking house of reflections
with words and their shadows).

These two lines are swollen with significance and are projected toward many sides: if words are being, their *shadows* are death (clashing contraries) and are linked with the notion of house (house of the dead, house in which he lived); house in movement however (new contradiction), which projects reflections—split, incarnated light. The poem is then, totality itself because it contains its contrary in the transitoriness of its sexual embrace

Espiral de los ecos, el poema
es aire que se esculpe y se disipa.

(Spiral of echoes, the poem
is air which sculpts itself and dissipates.)

At his incantation, the signs rotate and are ordered as in the solar system:

. . . las repúblicas
errantes de sonidos y sentidos,
en rotación magnética se enlazan y dispersan
sobre el papel.

236

(the wandering
republics of sounds and senses
in magnetic rotation connect and disperse
on the paper.)

We have reached the epilogue which opens with an agreement that we hear in the first and fourth parts:

Estoy en donde estuve

(I am where I was).

From that central position he perceives, as if they were others, the whispering and the steps he listened to "with his soul" on beginning the poem. Now he states that there are "steps inside me," that he hears them "with his eyes" and because

el murmullo es mental, yo soy mis pasos

(the murmur is mental, I am my steps).

The past is here, in this instantaneous midday in which light bursts like a fruit. Remaining behind were the deceptive tunnels, the dark wells, the fixed puddle of memory. The echoes are not echoes: they are

las voces que me piensan al pensarlas

(the voices who think of me on thinking of them).

The third line of the poem

sombras del pensamiento más que pasos

(shadows of thought more than steps)

is remembered and denied by the line that ends it, there is no longer any shadow other than consciousness itself, says this final line gravely:

Soy la sombra que arrojan mis palabras.

(I am the shadow that my words cast.)

in that dark irreducible reality the process is affirmed and brought to an end. And in that negation is found the essential meaning of the poem: all has already been past in clarity and consciousness remains silent so that its words may speak. The spiritual recognition ends with the *I*'s silence.

Coda

Three principal ideas of Paz's thought and creation—poetry conceived and practiced above all as an *experience;* language like an operation that expands over its own boundaries; and the search for a totality like an equilibrium between contrary meanings—have been displayed or reelaborated in three of Paz's most recent critical works. We find the first in *Conjunciones y disyunciones (Conjunctions and Disjunctions),* an indispensable book for understanding his connection with Oriental thought (Buddhism, Taoism, Tantrism). Speaking precisely of *mantras,* Paz opposes two completely distinct types of poetic language: that which predominates in the Christian West and that of the magic Indian formulas:

> ... opposed to the verbal simplicity of Protestant Christianity, enemy of all secret writings—a symbolic and hermetic language; opposed to a neutral and abstract moral vocabulary—genital words and phonetic and semantic copulations; opposed to prayers, sermons and the economy of a rational language—the jingle-like *mantras.* A language that distinguishes between the act and the word and, inside of the latter, between the signifier and the signification—another which erases the distinction between the word and the act ...
>
> *(CD, 85)*

This union between word and act is the nucleus of the *sacred* condition of poetry and the origin of its transcendental force. Absolute and even inconceivable powers of the word: Paz underscores this in his *Traducción: literatura y literalidad (Translation: Literature and the Literal),* which offers us another opposition: while the poem has many modes of meaning and these modes can change, the words which shape them are "unique and irreplaceable." It is made of words, but can't be reduced to them; that's why

La poesía, sin cesar de ser lenguaje, es un más
allá del lenguaje.[8]

(Poetry, without ceasing to be language, is beyond
language.)

Consequently, what poetry pursues is something that at once
it recognizes and does not recognize, what it has and what it
has lost. Restoring what humankind longs for in the same
way restores and expresses its necessity of something distinct.
A passage at the end of *El mono gramático*[9] says it with
greater clarity:

> Poetry does not want to know what lies at the journey's
> end: it conceives of the text as a series of translucent
> strati in whose interior the distinct parts—the different
> verbal and semantic currents—on intertwining or unravel-
> ing, reflecting or cancelling out, produce momentary
> configurations. Poetry searches for, contemplates, unites
> and cancels itself out in the crystalization of language.

The correspondence between these theoretical books of
Octavio Paz and the inquiry and discovery contained in *Pasado
en claro*, confirms the profound unity and consistency of his
vision, apart from showing the exact place this text occupies
within his work. Poetic theories, cultural reflections, inventive performance—all lead to that revelation of the memorable final line we can now better comprehend:

Soy la sombra que arrojan mis palabras.

(I am the shadow that my words cast.)

trans. from the Spanish by Kosrof Chantikian

---

[8] *El signo y el garabato* (Joaquín Mortiz: Mexico, 1973), p. 65.
[9] Seix Barral: Barcelona, 1974, p. 134.

Bernard Horn

HEARING OCTAVIO PAZ READ

Clear
without meaning, I rode his rhythms
into feeling,
the resonance, the warmth, the precision and humor of his voice
and his silences
into feeling—

his right hand
lightly punctuates or syncopates, fingers
relaxed or outspread, and sometimes just his thumb
counts the measure
barely moving in the loose fist
as the few
familiar sounds flicker
in my mind—

silencio

nieve

while you
heard the union
of rhythm and meaning, began
El presente
to turn
El presente es perpetuo
to me, moved
Los montes
by his lines, moved too to share them
El viento
and move with them,
El cielo . . .

tus ojos de agua humana
and once just as you began to
La lluvia
the clear unintelligible sounds
La lluvia no te moja
Eres la llama de agua
overflowed the room and I was
floating and I was water
and your moving
and its certainty fused
with the measure of his voice, his face,
his hand, your unseen eyes, and we were
one
(though I'm not sure you knew)

in his music,
in the silence that is music,
the silence that precedes
the quick intake of air
that precedes the realization
that we are many and we are
one,
that Claudia and Bernardo have had the privilege
to linger
in Octavio's imagination,

losing themselves in the shining water there
in Teotihuacán the city of the gods
where the modest Nanahuatzin, The Pimply One,
threw himself, stepped out of himself into
the sacred fire
to be consumed
and reborn
as the sun.

Hugo J. Verani

WORKS OF OCTAVIO PAZ*

Poetry

Luna silvestre. Mexico, 1933.

Raíz del hombre. Mexico: Simbad, 1937.

¡No pasarán! Mexico: Simbad, 1937.

Bajo tu clara sombra y otros poemas sobre España. Valencia: Ediciones Españolas, 1937. Note by Manuel Altolaguirre. 2nd ed. *Bajo tu clara sombra (1935-1938).* Mexico: Tierra Nueva, 1941.

Entre la piedra y la flor. Mexico: Nueva Voz, 1941; 2nd ed. Mexico: Ediciones Asociación Cívica Yucatán, 1956. In 1976, Paz rewrote the entire text; see *Vuelta* (Mexico), v. 1, no. 9 (August, 1977).

A la orilla del mundo y primer día, Bajo tu clara sombra, Raíz del hombre, Noche de resurrecciones. Mexico: Compañía Editora y Librera ARS, 1942.

Libertad bajo palabra. Mexico: Tezontle, 1949; *Libertad bajo palabra: obra poética* (1935-1957). Mexico: Fondo de Cultura Económica, 1960. Greatly expanded version of the 1949 ed. 2nd ed. 1968. This second edition omits more than forty pcems of the first and gathers together previously unedited poems or those which had appeared only in magazines.

¿Águila o sol? Mexico: Tezontle, 1951; also Mexico: Fondo de Cultura Económica, 1973.

Semillas para un himno. Mexico: Tezontle, 1954.

Piedra de sol. Mexico: Tezontle, 1957.

La estación violenta. Mexico: Fondo de Cultura Económica, 1958.

Agua y viento. Bogotá: Eds. Mito, 1959.

Salamandra (1958-1961). Mexico: Joaquín Mortiz, 1962.

Viento entero. Delhi: The Laxton Press, 1965.

Vrindaban, Madurai. Delhi: The Laxton Press, 1965.

Blanco. Mexico: Joaquín Mortiz, 1967; 2nd ed. 1972.

Discos visuales. Mexico: Ediciones Era, 1968.

Ladera este (1962-1968). Mexico: Joaquín Mortiz, 1969; 2nd ed. 1970; 3rd ed. 1975.

La centena (poemas 1935-1968). Barcelona: Barral Editores, 1969; 2nd ed. 1972.

Topoemas. Mexico: Ediciones Era, 1971.

Renga. Mexico: Joaquín Mortiz, 1972. A collective poem in four languages with: Jacques Roubaud, Eduardo Sanguineti and Charles Tomlinson.

---

*The following are all works published in book form. For a more comprehensive bibliography see Hugo Verani's "Hacia la bibliografía de Octavio Paz" in *Cuadernos Hispanoamericanos* (Madrid, Enero-Marzo, 1979), nos. 343-345, pp. 752-91; and Alfredo A. Roggiano's "Bibliography by and on Octavio Paz," in Ivar Ivask, ed. *The Perpetual Present: The Poetry and Prose of Octavio Paz* (Norman: University of Oklahoma Press, 1973), pp. 133-57. —Ed.

242

Pasado en claro. Mexico: Fondo de Cultura Económica, 1975. [2nd
revised ed. 1978 —Ed.]

Vuelta. Barcelona: Seix Barral, 1976.

Poemas (1935–1975). Barcelona: Seix Barral, 1979. Contains the complete poetical works of Paz with many poems appearing newly revised.

Prose

El laberinto de la soledad. Mexico: Cuadernos Americanos, 1950; 2nd
ed. revised and augmented, Mexico: Fondo de Cultura Económica,
1959; 8th ed. 1970.

✓*El arco y la lira: El poema. La revelación poética. Poesía e historia*. Mexico: Fondo de Cultura Económica, 1956; 2nd ed. revised, 1967; 3rd
ed. 1972.

✓*Las peras del olmo*. Mexico: Universidad Nacional Autónoma de Mexico,
1957; revised ed. Barcelona: Seix Barral, 1971; 2nd ed. 1974.

Cuadrivio. Mexico: Joaquín Mortiz, 1965; 3rd ed. 1972.

Los signos en rotación. Buenos Aires: SUR, 1975. In 2nd ed. of *El arco
y la lira*.

Puertas al campo. Mexico: Universidad Nacional Autónoma de Mexico,
1966; 2nd ed. 1967; another ed. Barcelona: Seix Barral, 1972.

Claude Lévi-Strauss o el nuevo festín de Esopo. Mexico: Joaquín Mortiz,
1967. 4th ed. 1975.

Corriente alterna. Mexico: Siglo Veintiuno Editores, 1967; 6th ed. 1972.

Marcel Duchamp o el castillo de la pureza. Mexico: Era, 1968.

Conjunciones y disyunciones. Mexico: Joaquín Mortiz, 1969.

Mexico: la última década. Austin, Texas: Institute of Latin American
Studies, University of Texas, 1969.

✓*Posdata*. Mexico: Siglo Veintiuno Editores, 1970; 8th ed. 1973.

✓*Las cosas en su sitio: sobre la literatura española del siglo XX* (in collaboration with Juan Marichal), Mexico: Finisterre, 1971.

Los signos en rotación y otros ensayos. Prologue and selection by Carlos
Fuentes. Madrid: Alianza Editorial, 1971.

Traducción: literatura y literalidad. Barcelona: Tusquets Editor, 1971.

Apariencia desnuda: la obra de Marcel Duchamp. Mexico: Ediciones
Era, 1973.

El signo y el garabato. Mexico: Joaquín Mortiz, 1973.

Solo a dos voces (in collaboration with Julián Ríos). Barcelona: Editorial
Lumen, 1973.

Teatro de signos/transparencias. Selection and montage by Julián Ríos,
Madrid: Editorial Fundamentos, 1974.

La búsqueda del comienzo. Madrid: Editorial Fundamentos, 1974.

El mono gramático. Barcelona: Seix Barral, 1974.

✓*Los hijos del limo: del romanticismo a la vanguardia*. Barcelona: Seix
Barral, 1974.

Xavier Villaurrutia en persona y en obra. Mexico: Fondo de Cultura Económica, 1978.

El ogro filantrópico: historia y política 1971–1978. Mexico: Joaquín
Mortiz, 1979.

In/mediaciones. Barcelona: Seix Barral, 1979.

Theater

La hija de Rappaccini. One act play, based on a short story by Nathaniel Hawthorne. *Revista Mexicana de Literatura,* v. 2, no. 7 (septiembre-octubre 1956).

Works in English Translation

The Labyrinth of Solitude: Life and Thought in Mexico. New York: Grove Press, 1962. Trans. by Lysander Kemp.

Sun Stone. New York: New Directions, 1973. Trans. by Muriel Rukeyser.

Sun-Stone. Toronto: Contact Press, 1963. Trans. by Peter Miller.

Selected Poems. Bloomington: Indiana University Press, 1963. Trans. by Muriel Rukeyser.

Piedra de sol. The Sun Stone. York: Cosmos Publications, 1969. Trans. by Donald Gardner.

Piedra de Sol. Sun Stone. Texas Quarterly, v. 13, no. 3 (Autumn, 1970). Trans. by Laura Villaseñor.

Marcel Duchamp: or, The Castle of Purity. London: Cape Goliard, 1970. Trans. by Donald Gardner.

Claude Lévi-Strauss: An Introduction. Ithaca: Cornell University Press, 1970. Trans. by J. S. Bernstein and Maxine Bernstein.

¿Águila o sol? Eagle or Sun? New York: October House, 1970; 2nd ed. New York: New Directions, 1976. Trans. by Eliot Weinberger.

Configurations. New York: New Directions, 1971, and London: Cape, 1971. Trans. by G. Aroul and others.

Renga: A Chain of Poems. New York: George Braziller, 1972. With Jacques Roubaud, Eduardo Sanguineti, Charles Tomlinson. Foreword by Claude Roy. Trans. by Charles Tomlinson.

The Other Mexico: Critique of the Pyramid. New York: Grove Press, 1972. Trans. by Lysander Kemp.

Early Poems 1935–1955. New York: New Directions, 1973 and Bloomington: Indiana University Press, 1974. Trans. by Muriel Rukeyser and others.

Alternating Current. New York: Viking Press, 1973. Trans. by Helen R. Lane.

The Bow and the Lyre: The Poem. The Poetic Revelation. Poetry and History. Austin: University of Texas Press, 1973. Trans. by Ruth L. C. Simms.

Blanco. New York: The Press, 1974. Introduction by Roger Shattuck and trans. by Eliot Weinberger.

Children of the Mire: Poetry from Romanticism to the Avant-garde. Cambridge: Harvard University Press, 1974. Trans. by Rachel Phillips.

Conjunctions and Disjunctions. New York: Viking Press, 1974. Trans. by Helen R. Lane.

The Siren and the Seashell and Other Essays on Poets and Poetry. Austin: University of Texas Press, 1976. Trans. by Lysander Kemp and Margaret Sayers Peden.

Marcel Duchamp: Appearance Stripped Bare. New York: Viking Press, 1978. Trans. by Rachel Phillips and Donald Gardner.

A Draft of Shadows and other Poems. New York: New Directions, 1979. Edited and trans. by Eliot Weinberger with additional trans. by Elizabeth Bishop and Mark Strand.

Anthologies

An Anthology of Mexican Poetry. Bloomington: Indiana University Press, 1958. Edited by Octavio Paz and translated by Samuel Beckett with a preface by C. M. Bowra.

New Poetry of Mexico. New York: Dutton, 1970; London: Secker & Warburg, 1972. Selection and notes by Octavio Paz, Alí Chumacero, José Emilio Pacheco and Homero Aridjis. Prologue by Octavio Paz. Edited by Mark Strand. This is the English version of *Poesía en movimiento.*

☆　　　　　☆　　　　　☆

CONTRIBUTORS

Jaime Alazraki lives in Cambridge, Mass. and teaches at Harvard.

Homero Aridjis lives in Mexico City and was Writer-in-Residence at Columbia University last year.

Yves Bonnefoy lives in Paris. *Dans le leurre du seuil (In the Lure of the Threshold)* is his most recent book of poems in verse.

John Cage lives in New York. He recently toured Europe with the Merce Cunningham Dance Company.

Kosrof Chantikian lives and works in San Francisco.

Manuel Durán has published several collections of his poetry. Some translations of his work by Willis Barnstone will appear in *KOSMOS* 7. He is chairman of Yale's Spanish Department.

Claude Esteban also lives in Paris and edits *Argile*. *KOSMOS* will soon publish his book of poems, *Transparent God*, in a bilingual edition.

Carlos Fuentes lives in Princeton, N.J. where he is working on a new novel. His major work is *Terra Nostra*, first published in Mexico in 1975.

Ricardo Gullón lives in Chicago where he teaches at the University of Chicago.

Harry Haskell is a translator presently living in Los Angeles.

Jack Hirschman, who lives in San Francisco, is on an extended trip through Europe. He is co-translator of *Electric Iron* by Vladimir Mayakovsky.

Edwin Honig lives and teaches in Providence, R.I. and is finishing his translation of Lope de Vega's *La Dorothea*. His *Selected Poems 1955–1976* appeared in 1979.

Bernard Horn lives in Cambridge, Mass.

Susanna Lang also lives in Chicago. She translated Yves Bonnefoy's *Pierre écrite (Words in Stone)*. Her poetry will appear in *KOSMOS* 7.

Robert Lima lives in Pennsylvania and teaches at Penn State.

Julio Ortega, a Poet from Peru, lives now in Austin, Texas. His *Tierra en el día* was published in English in 1978.

José Miguel Oviedo, also a Peruvian, lives in Bloomington, Indiana where he teaches at Indiana University.

Octavio Paz lives in Mexico City but we first met in Los Angeles three months ago.

Margaret Sayers Peden lives in Columbia, Missouri. She is currently translating Pablo Neruda's *Odas elementales.* Her other translations include Carlos Fuentes' *Terra Nostra.*

Allen W. Phillips lives and teaches in Santa Barbara, Calif.

Kenneth Rexroth lived in San Francisco for forty years and now also lives in Santa Barbara.

Anthony Rudolf lives in London.

José L. Varela-Ibarra and I first met in front of the San Francisco Public Library a few days after Christmas 1979. He will be in Miami for the coming year.

Hugo J. Verani lives and teaches in Davis, Calif.